Love

a world photography

———

a journey of understanding

www.inspirita.org

◄ inspirita ►

Inspirita, 12 Vale Road, Bowdon, Cheshire, UK WA14 3AQ
www.inspirita.org

ISBN 9 781909 204225

This book is produced on paper from sustainable managed forests

there is projection
there is denial
in between there is seeing

not the world that we desire
nor the world that we reject
but the world that is

the human creation
the natural environment
the wonder of the universe

an unconditional celebration
with mind heart soul
with camera
the same

to be free
to see it

as it is

to see is to love

Devotion   Varkala, Kerala   Jan 07

india   january

Becoming God   Katha Kali Theatre, Varkala, Kerala   Jan 10

God and Goddess   Katha Kali Theatre, Varkala, Kerala   Jan 10

Seeing The Light   Varkala, Kerala   Jan 09

The ritual of fire is a profound moment in any Indian ceremony. This moment, known as Darshan, literally means 'seeing'. It could be thought of as 'seeing God' or, as we might understand it in Western secular terms,' seeing the light'.

When the hands are brought together in the Indian greeting of 'Namaste', it signifies ' I pray to the God within you'. God is not seen as an object - the various spiritual symbols of Indian culture serve as gateways through which to access the godliness within.

Rite de Passage   Varkala, Kerala   Jan 09

From time immemorial, Indians have come to the sea shore at Varkala for the purpose of bidding farewell to their loved ones on their journey into the next incarnation.

During a short ceremony, a small package of rice, flowers and herbs is blessed and wrapped in a banana leaf. The mourner walks to the seashore and then facing away from the sea, throws the sanctified article over a shoulder.

The final stage of the ritual is to walk away with one's back towards the sea.......

Life Is A ....   Varkala, Kerala   Jan 07

Sajeer   Varkala, Kerala   Jan 10

Samsara   Varkala, Kerala   Jan 04

Literally meaning 'continuous flow' and often depicted as a whirlpool, the notion of Samsara encompasses the forces that suck a person deeper and deeper into the play of the senses, into the interminable actions of cause and effect and into continually defining oneself in relation to others - in other words, what most people would consider to be 'the world'.

Maya is the state of illusion whereby one takes Samsara, the play of the world, to be real. Liberation in the Indian spiritual tradition is the realisation that because everything is always interacting and changing its relationship with everything else, that nothing is real in Samsara.

Or more precisely that Samsara is 'apparent reality' and is neither real nor unreal - that is, 'the world' just appears to be real.

'It was all a game and a sham, all foam and dream. It was Maya, the whole lovely and frightful, delicious and desperate kaleidoscope of life with its searing delights, its searing griefs'

'The Indian Life'   The Glass Bead Game - Hermann Hesse 1943

You And Me   Varkala, Kerala   Jan 06

Boys   Mamallapuram, Tamil Nadu   Jan 20

Memento   Mamallapuram, Tamil Nadu   Jan 20

Intimacy   Mamallapuram, Tamil Nadu   Jan 20

Girls   Mamallapuram, Tamil Nadu   Jan 20

Sacred   Countryside, Tamil Nadu   Jan 17

Sand Painting   Tiruvannamalai, Tamil Nadu   Jan 14

During Pongal, the harvest festival of Tamil Nadu, the horns of the cattle are newly painted and the streets are adorned with paintings. The earth replenishes for another year.

Harvest Festival   Tiruvannamalai, Tamil Nadu   Jan 17

Flower Seller   Tirukovilur, Tamil Nadu   Jan 17

Fresh   Tirukovilur, Tamil Nadu   Jan 17

Indian Girl   Tirukovilur, Tamil Nadu   Jan 17

Coconuts   Tirukovilur, Tamil Nadu   Jan 17

Lunch Break   Tiruvanamalai, Tamil Nadu   Jan 19

Heavy Lifting   Tiruvanamalai, Tamil Nadu   Jan 19

'BRICS'   Countryside, Tamil Nadu   Jan 17

First coined in 2001 by Jim O'Neill of Goldman Sachs, the term BRICS (Brasil, Russia, India, China) became the acronym for a new category of investment in rapidly developing economies. The rate of economic growth in India since 2000 has been prodigious, averaging 7.4% pa, 2000-2012.

Other than major cataclysms (wars, revolutions, natural disasters etc), in the normal course of events, nothing changes societies faster than economic change. Though 700 million Indians live on $2 per day or less, there is now a growing middle class of more than 50 million Indians with disposable income ranging from $4,000-$21,000. Estimates are that the middle class will grow tenfold by 2025 and will lead to a huge European style consumer economy.

Another 80 million Indian people have been brought out of dire poverty in the decade and though definitions vary between various studies, they all seem to agree that since the 1970s about 250 million people have risen above the Indian poverty line, That still leaves a lot of poverty and the World Bank estimates that a third of the world's poor are resident in India.

The Cave   Tirukovilur, Tamil Nadu   Jan 17

The World and Spirituality

The various faiths, ideologies and belief systems of the world have for so long offered their own 'spiritual paths' that it is entirely commonplace to confuse religion with spirituality - nothing could be further from the truth. The essential point to grasp is that the faiths, laws, values and social rules that we see today all proceeded out of the womb of consciousness.

Our own inherent spirituality existed long before any of the faiths, belief systems or political ideologies came into existence. The faiths of the world are, in fact, spirituality taking form. This is why there is a unity of experience at the heart of all the world's faiths and values - they all come from the same place.

Secondly, although it may offer a route back to the source, as soon as spirituality takes a particular form, it has inevitably departed from the limitless spiritual domain from which it originated. When this is combined with the desires, fears and needs of the human being, a spiritual form almost invariably transforms into a mind set.

However laudable a mind set may be, what has happened is that our infinite and limitless nature has now become something finite and limited and therefore contrary to that original nature. Has any belief system, no matter how strict and austere, ever been able to stop the freedom of the spirit when it is dreaming?

Lastly, the Indian spiritual tradition has a very definite and clear purpose - to be free. This is not a pleasure seeker's charter for if desires, needs and the senses let rip, one would very rapidly find oneself in all manner of entanglements that are very un-liberating.   On the contrary, the purpose is to liberate oneself from anything that stands in the way of our limitless and infinite nature. And to be true to that nature.

Those so imbued with a particular point of view that they cannot imagine anything beyond the play of one ideology or another, would obviously have great difficulty in taking on board such a truly free notion of liberation - that there is a power within each human being greater than the power of social conditioning.

As the process of liberation eschews attachment to any particular point of view, the critique of the ideologue would typically be that such a liberation creates an 'ideology of viewlessness', of not having a point of view about anything. In actual fact, liberation is not 'viewlessness'; rather it is 'viewfullness' - that is that one is free to look at any situation from any number of points of view in order to come to a complete understanding of whatever is happening.

The camera in this project takes due note of such observations.

Never Too Old For Love   Tiruvannamalai, Tamil Nadu   Jan 18

You're never too old to find true love ! At a sprightly seventy years of age, James Swartz, from Montana, USA and a Vedanta teacher on the world spiritual circuit, and Isabella Vigletti, an artist from South Africa in her fifties, fell in love with each other and married a few months earlier. Ramana looks on beatifically.

James Swartz's Vedanta seminars (opposite) are well known for shining a witty, knowledgeable and often humourous light of truth at the whacky side of the world of spirituality.

Vedanta has a very simple definition of reality ; ' That which does not change '

This immediately cuts out huge chunks of what most people think of as 'the real world'. Socio-economic status is in a continuous state of flux, social rules and values are always adapting to advances in thought and changes in lifestyles etc, and scientific revelations continually break through the boundaries of consciousness etc etc.

What is it that does not change ? According to Vedanta, the fundamental reality behind all such changes is 'the self', otherwise defined as our inherent bedrock consciousness, the deep non-conceptual awareness that we are aware. It is through contact with 'the self' that one can cut through the wild noises of the day and live out one's life at a truer, deeper level.

What is Reality ?   Tiruvannamalai, Tamil Nadu   Jan 15

Ramana Ashram   Tiruvannamalai, Tamil Nadu   Jan 14

'realising one's true nature is liberation'

Ramana Maharsi

Who am I ?   Ramana Ashram Bookshop   Jan 20

Just because there are freedoms of speech, thought, worship and association etc, does not mean that the exercise of those freedoms will result in a free human being. One would, for example, like to think that the more religious a person becomes, the more tolerant they are. All too often, the opposite is the case - the more religious, the more intolerant. Nothing wrong with the faiths, nothing wrong with the prophets, but the way that human beings attach themselves to the faiths and the powerful organisations around them is in need of close examination.

Identity is the mechanism by which an individual becomes attached to a set of values. So the main issue with faith, or any other set of values, is that it gives a person an identity and therefore a defined view of the universe. Be it national, racial, political, social, economic, cultural, tribal, once a person has succumbed to an identity, they become susceptible to groupthink, to the trade off between social consensus and the truth, to what in this context might be termed 'the-self-censorship'.

As the human need for identity is also the basic building block for all forms of manipulation and exploitation, this in turn leads to many of the most destructive episodes in human history. And, as the process of dehumanisation begins at the point at which an idea or an identity is attached to, projected onto an otherwise free human being, the attachment of identity is, therefore, a critical matter.

There is hope in the realm of Human Rights and the Rule of Law but that is subject to the fact that people excel at demanding their rights and freedoms but fail miserably at extending those same rights and freedoms to others, especially to their ideological opposites. The way of human rights is a tough discipline and demands deep work on oneself. Unless one is free inside oneself, how can one extend that same freedom to others ? Unless one can transcend the world of identity, how can one begin the journey of freedom ?

What the Indian spiritual path asks for is not freedom of identity, but freedom from identity.

Mount Arunachala, sacred to Shiva, looms over Arunchalesvara Temple. Every Full Moon, hundreds of thousands of devotees gather to complete a barefoot thirteen kilometer pilgrimage around the base of the holy mountain - one of five Shiva Temples in Tamil Nadu which worship the five sacred elements :

Arunachulasvara   (Tiruvannamalai)   -   Fire
Jambukeswara   (Turichirappalli) -   Water
Ekambareswarar   (Kanchipuram)   -   Earth
Khalahasteeswara   (Srikalahasthi)   -   Air
Nataraja   (Chidambaram)   -   Space

The great temples of Tamil Nadu also bear witness to the wealth of the great Indian trading empires of the 5th to 15th centuries, which spread Indian spiritual culture across the rest of Asia. At its height the Chola empire controlled the bottom third of India, the coastal littoral and hinterland of India's east coast up to Burma, Sri Lanka, the Maldives, half of Borneo, the Malay peninsula, Sumatra and Java - why the 8th century Buddhist monument of Borobudur and the Hindu culture of Bali are found in present day Islamic Indonesia.

Fire   Arunachalesvara, Tiruvannamalai, Tamil Nadu   Jan 17

Ash   Arunachalesvara, Tiruvannamalai, Tamil Nadu   Jan 19

The three lines of ash symbolise that the three worlds have been reduced to ash.

The Gross, the Subtle and the Causal Worlds - that is 99% of what is in this weekend's Sunday newspapers - have been burned to ash in the fire of self knowledge.

So, look the gentleman straight in the eyes

Incline your forehead to the page

And proceed.................

Columbus Discovered America?   Chichen Itza, Yucatan   Feb 02

The Mayan civilisation was at its height from 250-900 AD, the Temple of Kukulkan (above)
being built in the Late Classical period, 750-850 AD. The Mayan people have survived and
the Mayan language is still spoken by millions to this day.

mexico   february

Zama (City Of Dawn)   Tulum, Quintana Roo   Feb 09

After the depopulation of many of the jungle sites, Zama (Tulum) flourished from the 13th to the
15th century as a port trading up and down the coastal regions of Central America and as a hub
of land and river routes into inland Guatemala and Mexico. Numerous artefacts have been found -
copper and flint, incense burners and gold objects, ceramics, salt, textiles, feathers and the most
prized of all, jade and obsidian. The obsidian would have to have traveled from Ixtepeque in
northern Guatemala, nearly 700 kilometers away. The site declined after contact with the
Spanish and by the end of the 16th century, Zama was abandoned completely.

Sacrifice   Nohoch Mul, Coba, Quintana Roo   Feb 10

For those who feel disinclined to don adventure wear disporting 30-40 zips and pockets per outfit and who do not require a ritual busting of the guts to feel that they are really traveling, Nohuch Mul, the tallest and steepest pyramid in the Yucatan, presents something of an issue - the large bottom in the green pants beached halfway up and one travel advisory suggested descending on one's posterior step by step. Health and Safety was not there at the dawn of consciousness in the Mayan world and every now and then whilst descending, a tourist will obligingly contribute to the pyramid's long history of human sacrifice.

Notwithstanding the ineradicable tabloid imagery of severed skulls and eviscerated gizzards lolloping and squidging their way down pyramids in Mel Gibson's 'Apocalypto', the Mayans had to first of all make sure that their sacrificial victims didn't peg out before actually getting to the top. No, Nohoch Mul was part of the lean machine Mayan Iron Man Commando training programme..... not for mere mortals who would prefer to start their day with a large latte...... a fromage frais...... a blueberry muffin........

Yucatan   Atop Nohoch Mul   Feb 10

Oaxaca   Surrounding Hills, Oaxaca   Feb 06

Everyday   Alcala, Oaxaca   Feb 05

Cafe Brujula   Alcala, Oaxaca   Feb 03

Inverse   Oaxaca   Feb 03

Obverse   Oaxaca   Feb 05

Panamas   Zocalo, Oaxaca   Feb 03

Sousaphones   Bandstand, Zocalo, Oaxaca   Feb 04

Oaxaca State Band   Zocalo, Oaxaca   Feb 05

Young Love   Zocalo, Oaxaca   Feb 03

Promenade   Zocalo, Oaxaca   Feb 05

Marimba   Zocalo, Oaxaca   Feb 05

Old Love   Zocalo, Oaxaca   Feb 05

Society   San Domingo, Oaxaca   Feb 04

Invitation   San Domingo, Oaxaca   Feb 04

Fashionista   San Domingo, Oaxaca   Feb 04

Oaxaquena Wedding   San Domingo, Oaxaca   Feb 04

Bridal Veil   San Domingo, Oaxaca   Feb 04

Casamiento / Marriage   San Domingo, Oaxaca   Feb 04

Bautizo / Baptism　　　　　Obispo Church, San Martin Tilcajete, Oaxaca　　　　　Feb 04

Father And Daughter   San Martin Tilcajete, Oaxaca   Feb 04

First Steps   San Martin Tilcajete, Oaxaca   Feb 04

Paseo De Bautizo   Obispo Church, San Martin Tilcajete, Oaxaca   Feb 04

Pueblo / Village   San Martin Tilcajete, Oaxaca   Feb 04

Cruz / Cross   Obispo Church, San Martin Tilcajete, Oaxaca   Feb 04

Many, many people in the world work very hard for very little. Here, this family is on its way to setting up a food stall outside the Police & Fire Stations.

Al Trabajo / To Work   Tulum, Quintana Roo   Feb 10

The huipil has been worn by indigenous women of Central Mexico and Central America, of both high and low social rank, since well before the arrival of the Spanish to the Americas. It remains the most common female indigenous garment still in use. It is decorated with designs that indicate the ethnicity and community of the wearer, as each have their own distinctive methods of creating and decorating the fabric.

Huipil   Valladolid, Yucatan   Feb 10

Youth   Valladolid, Yucatan   Feb 10

Family   Valladolid, Yucatan   Feb 10

Street Corner   Valladolid, Yucatan   Feb 10

'Each Day Is Valentine's Day....'   Zama's, Tulum, Quintana Roo   Feb 09

It being the time of year, Argentinian jazz singer Mariam Dedyn (opposite) pulls out
a magical rendition of the Rodgers & Hart classic, 'My Funny Valentine'

Zero Photoshop   Carr. Boca Paila, Tulum, Quintana Roo   Feb 09

Socialist Republic   Saigon Airport, Ho Chi Minh City   March 03

vietnam   march

Dictatorship Of The Proletariat   Peoples' Committee Building, Hoi An   March 07

Capitalist Imperialism   Outskirts, Ha Noi   March 21

Vietnamese Kings   My Son, Quang Nam   March 05

American Imperialism   Imperial Enclosure, Hue   March 09

'Those who would take over the earth
 And shape it to their will
 Never, I notice, succeed'

Tao Teh Ching

Tranquillity   Tu Hieu Monastery, Hue   March 10

Thich Nhat Hanh

Should anyone ever have wondered why at the height of the Viet Nam war in 1966, a local Zen Buddhist monk, Thich Nhat Hanh, went on a peace mission to the United States, then one need do no other than to walk through the entrance of the Tu Hieu Monastery. From such a haven of tranquillity, the napalming and carpet bombing of Viet Nam by American bombers must have seemed particularly grotesque.

Nhat Hanh entered Tu Hieu Monastery at the age of 16 and was ordained as a monk in 1948. Citing, as an example of the individual's active role in promoting change, the 13th century Vietnamese Emperor, Tran Nhan Tong, who abdicated his throne to become a monk, Nhat Hanh became an engaged Buddhist and a peace activist. He edited Buddhist publications, founded the Van Hanh Buddhist university and set up a corps of Buddhist peace-workers in rural Viet Nam. After completing studies at Princeton from 1960-1963, he returned to Viet Nam to aid his fellow monks in their non-violent peace efforts. At a meeting in April 1965, the Van Hanh students issued a Call for Peace : "It is time for North and South Vietnam to find a way to stop the war and help all Vietnamese people live peacefully and with mutual respect." Nhat Hanh left for the U.S. shortly afterwards to denounce the American involvement in Viet Nam and in 1967, Dr Martin Luther King nominated Thich Nhat Hanh for the Nobel Peace Prize stating : "I do not personally know of anyone more worthy .... than this gentle monk from Viet Nam. His ideas for peace, if applied, would build a monument to ecumenism, to world brotherhood, to humanity."

Continuous post war Vietnamese governments have taken a persistently strong line to those who either sided with the Americans or did not toe the party line. Accordingly, Nhat Hanh was banned from returning to Viet Nam for over thirty years from 1973-2005. Whilst being exceptionally well known in the West as a Buddhist teacher and commentator, Nhat Hanh has been ever mindful of the divisions that afflict his own country.

Engaged Buddhist   Tu Hieu Monastery, Hue   March 10

Rain Drops   Tu Hieu Monastery, Hue   March 10

Drifting Smoke   Tu Hieu Monastery, Hue   March 10

The Buddha   Thien Mu Pagoda, Hue   March 10

Saturday Night In Viet Nam - I   Downtown Hue   March 10

Saturday Night In Viet Nam - II   Downtown Hue   March 10

Potatoes   Tran Phu, Hoi An   March 05

Busy Man   Central Hoi An   March 07

Unruly Mob   Ha Long City, Quang Ninh   March 20

At an early stage in the visit to Viet Nam, this project very nearly came to a premature conclusion
when the camera was crossing a road in Hoi An on the naive assumption that the motor bike that
was travelling at 40 km/hr on the inside of the wrong side of the road could not possibly be there.

We have long advised clients to India on the only two rules of the Indian Highway Code :
1. Most of the time vehicles drive on the left. 2. If it's bigger than you, get out of the way.

Possibly a deep unconscious reaction to an authoritarian society and OK the country does have
35 million 125cc motor bikes on its overcrowded roads but for Viet Nam we have to add a third rule :
3. Expect anybody to do anything. As anybody does anything they want on the roads, the only way
to survive is to expect them to do precisely that.

Or is it that old dictum that someone's real personality comes out when they get behind the steering
wheel ? The Myth of the Noble Comrade ?

Tailor Made   Nguyen Thai Hoc, Hoi An   March 05

Check Out   Quy Nhon, Binh Dinh   March 13

Fisherman   Ha Long Bay, Quang Ninh   March 18

'Happy Woman Day'   International Women's Day, Hoi An   March 08

Asian Tigers   Halong City   March 19

Asian Cookers   Miss Ly Cafe, Hoi An   March 09

Ao Dai   Tran Phu, Hoi An   March 06

Dan Tranh   Tran Phu, Hoi An   March 06

Mostly performed by female musicians in Ao Dai (traditional Vietnamese dress) and typically used to accompany poetry recitals, the 17 string Dan Tranh has become a popular instrument throughout Viet Nam. The left hand plucks the strings while the right hand regulates the pitch and vibrato.

Together with flute accompaniment, the Hoi An Poetry Society recital proceeded at a high level of performance - the timing and singing was really quite professional.

Poetry Society   Tran Phu, Hoi An   March 06

Superstition   Full Moon, Tran Phu, Hoi An   March 06

Fruit   Full Moon, Tran Phu, Hoi An   March 06

Origin
Tram Ton Pass, Lao Cai
March 16

Exploitation   Song Hong River, Lao Cai   March 17

Rice Terraces   Sa Pa, Lao Cai   March 16

Buffalo   Countryside, Lao Cai   March 17

Every Grain Of Rice   Countryside, Yen Bai   March 17

Scoffing down a bowl of rice without thinking, it is hard to realise the often back-breaking human effort that has been taken in getting that rice to our tables. Every stage, from the buffalo trudging through the mud to the rice packet on our supermarket shelves, is a process worthy of absolute respect. The same applies to all objects, a huge amount of human energy is devoted to the material creation. Rice, of course, is an absolute necessity but as Adam Smith pointed out over two hundred years ago, 'trinkets of frivolous utility' are just as important in maintaining the momentum of the world economy.

Fortunately rice is an internationally tradable commodity for which, as there are rice paddies from the top to the bottom of the country, Viet Nam is ideally suited. As China (130 mn tns) and India (95 mn tns) consume almost all their own rice, and as most countries prefer different types of rice, of the 450 mn tns produced annually, less than 10% is traded, Thailand is traditionally the largest exporter of rice (11mn tns) but Viet Nam (7 mn tns) is now close behind, exporting about 25% of its crop. This is a huge turnaround from the near famine conditions of the 1980's as Viet Nam emerged out of Mao style farm collectivisation and, just like China, then allowed supply and demand to determine the outcome.

Tender Shoots   Countryside, Yen Bai   March 17

Ripening Grain   Qui Nhon, Binh Dinh   March 14

Truck Threshing   Countryside, Binh Dinh   March 13

Gathering In   Countryside, Binh Dinh   March 13

Vietnamese Girl   Countryside, Binh Dinh   March 13

To Rome With Love   Trastevere Multiplex, Rome   April 20

Woody Allen's latest film world premiered on the camera's first day in Italy.

italy   april

Built at public expense during the intense famine of 1646-48 and requiring the Piazza Navona to be cleared of its market traders, the building of Bernini's Fontana dei Quatro Fiumi flew in the face of opposition. When finally unveiled in 1651, the public was 'enraptured' by the great work - the four river gods, the Nile for Africa, the Danube for Europe, the Ganges for Asia and the Platte for the Americas, supporting an ancient Egyptian obelisk requisitioned by Emperor 'enemy of mankind' Caracalla c.200 AD, not to deny it its full provenance.

Gian Lorenzo Bernini   Piazza Navona, Rome   April 23

The awarding of the commission by Pope Innocent X was a matter of great intrigue, as Baldinucci's contemporary account reveals : ' Prince Niccolò Ludovisi, whose wife was niece to the Pope, persuaded Bernini to prepare a model of the fountain, and arrange for it to be secretly installed in a room in the Palazzo Pamphili that the Pope had to pass. On seeing such a noble creation, the Pope stopped almost in ecstasy. Being prince of the keenest judgment and the loftiest ideas, after admiring it, he said: "This is a trick ... It will be necessary to employ Bernini in spite of those who do not wish it, for he who desires not to use Bernini's designs, must take care not to see them."

Salvi / Bracci / Pannini   Trevi Fountain, Rome   April 23

The Sound Of The World   Piazza Della Rotunda, Rome   April 23

Day Market   Campo De Fiori, Rome   April 23

A Perfect Obsession   Via Baullari, Rome   April 20

Armani   Concourse, Venice   April 30

Evening Falls   Campo De Fiori, Rome   April 23

Well, It Is Italy...   Campo De Fiori, Rome   April 23

The World And Rock And Roll   Piazza Della Rotunda, Rome   April 22

Whilst no-one should feel shy about objecting to incessant busking whilst eating,
nevertheless the street musicians of Rome do have their moments. Marcello's perfect
rendition of Dire Straits' 'Sultans of Swing' in the Piazza Navona, an audience held
spellbound by a classically trained opera tenor one evening in the Piazza Della Rotunda,
or Vivaldi's Four Seasons drifting across the sensuous afternoon summer air ....

Here, a very useful guitar outfit run through the international standards : Pink Floyd,
Led Zeppelin, REM, Eric Clapton, Sting, Dylan, Eagles etc....... and thirty five years after
he became a Muslim and changed his name to Yusuf Islam, the world still hums along to
Cat Stevens' 'Father And Son' .

The World And Food
The Great Achievement - The Continuing Struggle

Forty years ago, in the late 1960s, in a world that was unable to feed its then world population of 3.7 billion, many of whom were living in dire third world poverty, projected rates of population growth against rates of food production confidently predicted imminent mass global starvation. It didn't happen - why was that ?

Recent FAO estimates indicate that in order to meet the projected demand for the next forty years, world food production in 2050 would need to increase by 60% above the level of 2005-07. There are grounds for optimism - in the last 40 years between 1961-63 and 2007-09, world food production increased by a massive 170%. Most of the growth originated from increases in yield and higher cropping intensity and this is expected to continue albeit at diminishing rates. Yield gains originated from improved cropping techniques, fertilisation and irrigation and much more is considered achievable by reducing wastage and post harvest losses, with the ultimate objective of narrowing the gap between experimental yields and actual farm yields. China's major rice producing regions have already achieved a very impressive 80% actual yield vs experimental yield.

For the world as a whole, per capita food availability has risen from about 2220 kcal/person/day in the early 1960s to 2790 kcal/person/day in 2006-08, while developing countries even recorded a leap from 1850 kcal/person/day to over 2640 kcal/person/day. This growth in food availability helped reduce the percentage of chronically undernourished people in developing countries from 34 percent in the mid 1970s to just 15 percent three decades later.

There have been significant external issues, land usage, mineral fertilisation, carbon emissions and great environmental pressure, but the overall world food situation has to be recognised for what it is - as a great achievement of mankind. Just think for one moment what would have happened if those 1960s projections had proven to be right ?

The razor's edge nature of existence guarantees that there is not one iota of room for complacency - not least in the fact that up to 1 billion people in the present day world are undernourished. Despite restrictions on land availability and freshwater resources, the FAO's view is that the gap is bridgeable by increasing yields, even within existing technology. The required increases in yield, land and irrigation will not come about spontaneously by relying solely on market forces, but will require considerable public intervention and investment, particularly in agricultural research and in preventing and mitigating environmental damage. The great driving force has been and will be the market but it is equally a legitimate matter of public policy. For example, it is strikingly obvious that the world has an overwhelming need for many more water reservoirs. In short, meeting the problem of world under-nourishment requires another huge collective human effort.

Lastly and returning to the achievement side of the equation, when next in an average western supermarket, stashed with its bewildering abundance of foods, drinks, sweets and spices from every corner of the planet - hallelujah, it's incredible - just think of the scene in Quentin Tarantino's film 'Pulp Fiction', where Samuel L Jackson has six or seven bullets fired at him, all of which miss him but which perfectly outline his body and which he memorably describes as 'a ****ing miracle'. This is completely analogous to the world food situation of the last forty years, for the world has been shot at and has only very narrowly escaped. And Samuel L Jackson's epithet applies exactly.

Siesta   Terlizzi, Puglia   April 22

Passeggiata   Via Sparano, Bari, Puglia   April 21

Centro Storico   Cathedral of San Sabino, Bari, Puglia   April 21

Centro Moderno   Ruvo Di Puglia, Puglia   April 22

Alley Chat   Pienza, Toscana   April 25

Val D'Orcia   Pienza, Toscana   April 25

Urban Space   il Campo, Siena, Toscana   April 26

Primal   Valdimontone Contrada, Siena, Toscana   April 26

A contrada is a district, or a ward, within an Italian city. The most well-known contrade are probably the 17 contrade of Siena that race in the Palio di Siena. Each is named after an animal or symbol and each with its own long history and complicated set of heraldic and semi-mythological associations. Set up in the Middle Ages to supply troops to the many military companies hired to defend Siena from Florence and other nearby city states, the contrade lost their administrative and military functions over time and became areas of localized patriotism, held together by the emotions and civic pride of the residents.

Their roles have broadened so that every important event – baptisms, deaths, marriages, church holidays, victories at the Palio, even wine or food festivals – is celebrated only within one's own contrada. Every contrada has its own museum, fountain and baptismal font, motto, allied contrada and adversary contrada. Often the adversary contrade share borders. Valdimontone (Ram) is situated in the south-east of the city near Porta Romana. Traditionally, its residents were tailors. It is allied with Onda (Wave) and is opposed to Nicchio (Shell) its neighbour. Onda and Valdimontone won the two most recent Palio races in 2012.

All sporting enthusiasts are familiar with career statistics and club records. As the modern Palio stretches back to 1656, the current all time winners are Oca (Goose) with 64 victories as against Aquila (Eagle) with only 24 victories. The title 'nonna' (grandmother) is bestowed on the contrada with the longest losing streak, currently Lupa (She-Wolf) without a victory since 1989.

Tribal   il Campo, Siena, Toscana   April 26

Early Morning   Grand Canal, Venice   April 30

Stillness   Rio Della Toletta, Venice   April 29

April 30   Grand Canal, Venice   'Whoever is Lord of Malacca.....

This is a very tough call and one that might ruffle some of the world's most precious aesthetic plumage but what you are really, really looking at in this picture is the Wall Street and Hudson River of the 13th to 16th centuries.

Strategically situated at the head of the Adriatic Sea, Venice developed extensive trade relations with the Byzantine Empire, the Muslim world and Europe. By the late 13th century, Venice had become the most prosperous city in all of Europe. At the peak of its power and wealth, it had 36,000 sailors operating 3,300 ships, dominating Mediterranean commerce. In building its maritime commercial empire, Venice monopolized the trade in salt, acquired control of many Aegean islands, including Cyprus and Crete, and became a major power-broker in the Near East. During this time, Venice's leading families vied with each other to build the grandest palaces and support the work of the greatest and most talented artists.

.....shall have his hands on the throat of Venice'   Grand Canal, Venice   April 28

Equally strategically located at the narrowest point between Sumatra and the Malay Peninsula, Malacca developed rapidly during the 15th century as a well equipped and well managed commercial port with facilities for warehousing cloves, nutmeg and mace from the Spice Islands and for cotton textiles from ports around the Indian ocean.. With an ethnically diverse and cosmopolitan merchant population, it was said that 84 different languages were spoken in Malacca during its heyday.

By the 15th century, Europe had developed an insatiable appetite for spices, essential for flavouring and preserving meats. The spice trade was monopolized by Venetian merchants via a convoluted trade route through Arabia and India, which in turn linked it to the Spice Islands via Malacca. John II, King of Portugal determined to break this chain and control the lucrative spice trade directly from its source. Pioneered by Vasco da Gama, Portuguese sea exploration expanded eastwards and in 1511 a fleet set sail from their naval base in Goa with 18 ships and 1,400 men to lay siege and eventually conquer Malacca. Despite local resistance and severe retaliation from Imperial China, the sea route to India and eastwards was established, destroying Venice's land route monopoly in the process. France, England and Holland soon followed.

Fresco   Grand Canal. Venice   April 30

Palazzo   Grand Canal. Venice   April 27

Gondola   Grand Canal. Venice   April 27

Primavera   Chiesa San Vidal, Venice   April 29

Though relatively well known across Europe in his lifetime, the brightness of Vivaldi's music is quintessential 'La Serenissima'. Born Antonio Lucio Vivaldi in Venice in 1678, he spent much of his working life there. At the age of 25, he worked at the Ospedale della Pietà, one of four institutions in Venice whose purpose was to give shelter and education to children who were abandoned or orphaned, or whose families could not support them. They were financed by funds provided by the Republic. The boys learned a trade and had to leave when they reached 15. The girls received a musical education, and the most talented stayed and became members of the Ospedale's renowned orchestra and choir. For composing two concerti and giving five rehearsals a month for the Ospedale, Vivaldi received two zecchinos, Venetian gold coins worth about $200 each at 2012 gold prices.

As performed above by Interpreti Veneziani, Le Quattro Stagioni (The Four Seasons) is his most famous work,

but he also composed 500 concerti and 46 operas, plus a large body of sacred choral music, sinfonias, sonatas and chamber music. Johann Sebastian Bach was certainly influenced by Vivaldi's works and transcribed six of Vivaldi's concerti for other instruments. During the height of his career, Vivaldi received commissions from European nobility and royalty but like many composers of the time, and as throughout the history of music, changing musical tastes meant Vivaldi's compositions became held in less high esteem and the final years of his life found him in financial difficulties. Vivaldi died in Vienna and was buried in poverty, his music becoming largely unknown to succeeding generations.

That we are able to appreciate and enjoy Vivaldi's music in the present day is largely down to certain key musicians and afficionados in the early 20th century who orchestrated a Vivaldi revival. The world has much to thank them for.

Once one has succumbed to the magic of Venice (that is, become completely oblivious of the other 60,000 tourists there every day) and once one has finally abandoned the last vestiges of reality (that is, put everything on one's credit card), then one can truly enter through the hallowed portals of the 'Republic of the Serenissima'

String quartets reverberate in the choral chambers of medieval churches, Cannaregio, Dorsoduro, enchanting quieter localities, a Veneto wedding takes place on the Grand Canal, and all the time the captivating rhythm of the world and its peoples and its extraordinary history deeply reflecting on itself.

La Serenissima   Chiesa San Vidal, Venice   April 29

Tourists, Tourists Everywhere   Grand Canal / Rio Da Scoacamini, Venice   April 30

Laundry   Canal Di Cannaregio, Venice   April 30

OMT !   Trump Tower, Chicago   May 19

united states   may

Steel And Water   Waterfront, Chicago   May 19

The Venice of the 2500s ?

Water And Steel   Chicago River, Chicago   May 19

NATO   Protest, Grant Park, Chicago   May 20

Bankers   Protest, Grant Park, Chicago   May 20

Planet   Protest, Grant Park, Chicago   May 20

Austerity   Protest, Grant Park, Chicago   May 20

Afghanistan / Israel   Protest, Grant Park, Chicago   May 20

Asia-Pacific   Protest, Grant Park, Chicago   May 20

Climate / Coal   Protest, Grant Park, Chicago   May 20

Third World   Protest, Grant Park, Chicago   May 20

Ashamed   Protest, Grant Park, Chicago   May 20

NATO / G8

To use a riposte of Bob Dylan's when being harangued into being a 'protest singer', would Chicago live up to its reputation as the 'protestiest' city in the United States? Considering the epic protests in Grant Park and on the streets of Chicago during the Democratic Convention of August 1968, there was good reason to think so. Barack Obama, President and a Chicago man, certainly thought so, he cancelled the G8 gathering in Chicago and transferred it to the high security retreat of Camp David, the NATO conference alone remaining in Chicago.

It had the intended effect. Had the G8 conference taken place in Chicago, the response would have been massive and international. As it was, even though CNN and the networks huffed and puffed to find a story and even though there were many striking images, nevertheless it was very nearly a total embarrassment for the organisers - 5,000-7,000 protesters would not be an overestimate.

Not that the organisers did themselves any favours once the faithful were gathered - in blistering 35C heat, the demo was preceded by a two hour long mind numbing barrage of radical epithets straight from the Fidel Castro and Hugo Chavez School of Oratory. To say that it made watching paint dry look interesting might perhaps be an exaggeration, but anyone with any sense (most everybody there) headed for the shade of the trees and sat it out.

A huge modern city was brought to a near-standstill, there were road blocks and police squads all over town, the Chicago Art Institute was closed for three days (not least for a frocks and canapes private viewing event for Michelle Obama and the NATO ladies) and half of Chicago grabbed a couple of extra days off, excellently timed for the first hot weather of the summer.

But the point was made (just). Those that braved the heat and the hassles (and ignored the oratory) raised the banner for the many millions that hold aloft the same placards.

The Protestiest City   NATO / G8 Protest, Michigan Avenue, Chicago   May 20

Night And The City   Downtown, Chicago   May 19

America On A Saturday Night   Kingston Mines Blues Club, Chicago   May 19

Central to the Las Vegas experience is the notion of making 'a nobody' feel like 'a somebody'.
This was exactly the opposite of the experience of the camera.

Gambling While America Burns   Las Vegas, Nevada   May 21

For consuming far more than it produces for far too long, the United States of America has contracted a deadly strain of the Debt virus, a terminal condition. The 'We are the greatest' rhetoric is a sham. As Bill Clinton put it at the Democratic Convention of August 2012 : 'The old economy is not coming back'. Though one cannot entirely predict 'events' and though many American citizens will live off their accumulated wealth for generations to come, the overwhelming diagnosis is that the Asia-Pacific region will now inherit the mantle of leadership of the world economy.

What we are witnessing are the pleasure seeking death throes of a busted flush. It happened to Rome. It happened to Britain. It is happening to America. No Empire can survive long, once its economic foundations have been undermined. It is now only a question of time.

The Fall Of The American Empire   Caesar's Palace, Las Vegas, Nevada   May 21

Wordless   Bright Angel Point, North Rim, Grand Canyon, Arizona   May 22

Timeless   Valhalla Overlook, North Rim, Grand Canyon, Arizona   May 23

Prayer   South Rim, Grand Canyon, Arizona   May 23

Worship   Valhalla Overlook, North Rim, Grand Canyon, Arizona   May 24

Arizona   Vermillion Cliffs, Arizona   May 24

Hacienda   Acoma, New Mexico   May 24

Homestead   McCarthys, New Mexico   May 24

New Mexico   Enchanted Mesa, Acoma, New Mexico   May 25

Studio   Santa Fe, New Mexico   May 27

Adobe   Santa Fe, New Mexico   May 27

Over 120 Galleries   Canyon Road, Santa Fe, New Mexico   May 27

Artist's Palette   Kathryn Stedham, Galisteo, New Mexico   May 27

Abstract I

Kathryn Stedham, Galisteo, New Mexico

Abstract II

Sunday Brunch   Harry's Roadhouse, Santa Fe, New Mexico   May 27

Pueblo Church   Taos Pueblo, Taos, New Mexico   May 26

Price Of Gas   Taos, New Mexico   May 26

The World And Oil

Regular Gas Price	Dollars Per Gallon
March 2000	$ 1.50
Feb 2005	$ 1.86
May 2007	$ 3.00
July 2008	$ 4.17
Jan 2009	$ 1.61
Jan 2010	$ 2.61
June 2011	$ 3.97
May 2012	$ 3.70

2011 - was the first year since records began that the US economy had less jobs than 10 years previously, 132mn down to 131mn.. In addition, every 2 year period since 1969 has previously seen a rise in per capita real disposable income in the US. 2011 was the first time this had not happened, over $33,000 in 2009 down to under $33,000 in 2011.

Nothing demonstrates more clearly the restructuring of the world economy in the 21st century and the relative economic decline of the USA, than the fact that the price of oil continued to rise throughout 2011 at a time of dire economic crisis for the US and Europe.

In such a situation, the price of oil would normally have come down. Sustained economic growth in the newly developing countries, the Asian tigers, Australia and above all China ensured that the world oil price has been brutally indifferent to the fate of the old economies.

2008 - that the rise in oil prices caused the 2008 recession might be to put it too strongly. However, as an 80 cent rise in pump prices takes $100bn or 1% out of disposable income, the fact that gas prices had doubled by the first signs of recession in 2007 meant that $200bn / 2% had already been sucked out of US household budgets. The price of gas then spiralled out of control from 2007 to 2008, household budgets were hammered by 3% plus losses ($150-$200 per month per employed person) and whilst not the only factor, the rise in the oil price must have contributed significantly to household mortgage defaults.

In the 2000s, US households and indeed the world consumer, took on levels of debt at sub-Neanderthal levels of intelligence. At no higher an IQ level, three post war generations of self-serving spendthrift politicians of all complexions littered the post war world with horrendous national debts.. But ultimately the trail of blood from the 2000s boom and bust runs straight across the noisy fish market of bankers and financiers and right up to the doors of the world's Central Banks, the world's Financial Regulators and the world's Finance Ministers and Ministries. They had the knowledge and the powers to anticipate, control and prevent the crash happening. Hence, the ultimate question : Why did the regulators not regulate ?

2012 onwards - when next filling a vehicle with fuel, spare a thought for the poor unfortunates that are the beneficiaries of your largesse.. If the oil price drops below $78 barrel, then Saudi Arabia would not be able to commandeer the $300bn pa that it needs to spend on the social projects that have soared since uprisings spread across the Arab world. Had the late Comrade Hugo Chavez lost control of the various unaudited oil funds, which as President he managed at his own discretion, then that might have loosened his grip on the government expenditure that rocketed by 26% before Venezuela's October 2012 Election. Not to mention Vladimir Putin's KGB stashed regime screwing Europe through Gazprom price fixing, Ahmadinejad's nuclear Iran, corrupt government officials siphoning off Nigeria's oil wealth and last but not least, the oil based sovereign wealth funds : Qatar $115 bn, Russia $150 bn, Kuwait $296 bn, Saudi Arabia $596 bn, the UAE $817 bn.... and Norway $664 bn !!! Now, what's a bunch of Scandinavian goodie-goodies doing amongst this lot ? Hardly surprising in this company that they gave the 'Petroleum Fund Of Norway' a makeover in 2005 - subsequently titled 'The Government Pension Fund Of Norway'.

Bikes   Taos, New Mexico   May 26

Babes   Taos, New Mexico   May 26

Heroes   Taos, New Mexico   May 26

Harleys   Taos, New Mexico   May 26

Memorial Weekend Rally   Red River, New Mexico   May 26

As the United States is so vilified in so many parts of the world, it might come as something of a shock to see that Americans love their country just as much as anyone else loves theirs - flag flying is pretty ubiquitous in the States.

Those that chafe at the thought of American patriotism should first of all check out their own patriotic credentials. If there is a criticism, it is that patriotism itself is an unworthy receptacle of human affection, leading to far too many destructive outcomes. Once one accepts patriotism per se, then one man's nationalism is another man's antagonism.

Up to a point, 'ra-ra-ing' the national sports teams is harmless and good fun, not to be taken too seriously so, win or lose, we can all enjoy the human spectacle. But the flags flying below are altogether of a more serious nature - to commemorate the fallen in war and the veterans that have survived, and why the bikers have gathered at this time. Just because it is the United States, one could get very disputatious very quickly. Perhaps one might look at it another way: every victory in war is a funeral and every person killed a tragedy.

Love Of Country   Questa, New Mexico   May 26

North

' Nothing ever comes to an end. Wherever one has sunk roots that
emanate from one's best or truest self, one will always find a home.'

Liv Ullmann

norway   june

Midsummer Evening   Finnoyen, Lofoten   June 21

'Anyone who wishes to fully understand me must know Norway..

The spectacular but severe landscape which people have around them in the North and the lonely
shut off life - the houses often lie miles from each other - force them not to bother about other
people, but only their own concerns, so that they become reflective and serious, they brood and doubt
and often despair. And those dark winters with the thick mist outside. Ah - they long for the sun!'

Henrik Ibsen

Expanse   By Reine, Lofoten   June 22

'His soul grew big inside him'   Knut Hamsun

Old White   Skrova, Lofoten   June 19

Awesome   Reine, Lofoten   June 23

What, then, is love? A wind whispering among the roses - no, a yellow phosphorescence in the blood. *A danse macabre* in which even the oldest and frailest hearts are obliged to join. It is like the marguerite which opens wide as night draws on, and like the anemone which closes at a breath and dies at a touch. Such is love. It can ruin a man, raise him up again, then brand him anew. Such is its fickleness it can favour me today, tomorrow you, tomorrow night a stranger. But such also is its constancy it can hold fast like an inviolable seal, can blaze unquenched until the hour of death. What, then, is the nature of love?

Ah, love is a summer night with stars in the heavens and fragrance on earth. But why does it cause the young man to follow secret paths, the old man to stand on tiptoe in his lonely chamber? Alas, it is love which turns the human heart into a fungus garden, a lush and shameless garden wherein grow mysterious, immodest toadstools.

Does it not cause the monk to creep by night through high-walled gardens and fasten his eye to the windows of sleepers? Does it not possess the nun with foolishness and darken the princess's understanding? It lays low the king's head by the wayside so that his hair sweeps the wayside dust as he whispers lewd words to himself and laughs and sticks out his tongue. Such is the nature of love.

No, no, it is something different again, like nothing else in the world. It visits the earth on a night in spring when a young man sees two eyes, two eyes. He gazes, he sees. He kisses a mouth, and it feels as though two lights have met in his heart, a sun that flashes at a star. He falls in her arms, and for him the whole world becomes silent and invisible.

Love was God's first word, the first thought that sailed across his mind. He said, Let there be light, and there was love. And every thing that he had made was very good, and nothing thereof did he wish unmade again. And love was creation's source, creation's ruler... but all love's ways are strewn with blossoms and blood, blossoms and blood.

'Victoria'   Knut Hamsun - 1898

Madonna   Edvard Munch   1894

Ropes   Kamøyvaer, Magerøy   June 25

Tackle   Finnoyen, Lofoten   June 21

Slowly   Tind, Lofoten   June 22

The Captain   Henningsvaer, Lofoten   June 23

The Crew   Henningsvaer, Lofoten   June 23

The Catch   Henningsvaer, Lofoten   June 23

Fish Racks   Henningsvaer, Lofoten   June 20

Dried Fish   Henningsvaer, Lofoten   June 20

Factory   Moskenes, Lofoten   June 22

Scavenging   Kamøyvaer, Magerøy   June 25

Stacked   Sørvågen, Lofoten   June 21

Boyhood Home   Hamsund, Hamarøy   June 19

Hamsun Centre   Presteid, Hamarøy   June 19

Art & Politics

'Fascism aestheticizes Politics, Communism politicizes Art' is a well know dictum in the intense debate about the relationship between Art & Politics. Is the best way for an Artist to contribute to stay true to their Art? Should well known Artists use their position to promote political points of view? Or would a really pure Artist not even think about the effect of their work in the first place?

'When religion and politics mix, you get politics,' could the same be said about Art, the more the politics, the less the Art?

There it is - Knut Hamsun, awarded the Nobel Prize for Literature in 1920, feted in literary circles across Europe throughout the 20s and 30s and then stripped of all his possessions and committed to an asylum, having supported Hitler and the Nazis during World War II. In 1943 he presented his Nobel Medal to Minister of Propaganda, Joseph Goebbels and in 1945 on the news of Hitler's death, submitted a glowing obituary to one of Norway's main newspapers. Considered to be one of the founders of the 'stripped down' 'dead-on word' style of modern literature, to be the Kafka before Kafka, his books were burned and he became 'the most hated man in Norway'. The statement on the wall of the Hamsun Centeret captures the dilemma exactly :

'How could Hamsun, who wrote so beautifully of Love and Life, give his support to such a malevolent regime?'

The assumption that all artists hold liberal humanitarian views is counter-factual, many artists and celebrities support conservative and right wing causes. Nevertheless the post war critique that Nazism occurred in the then most cultured nation of Germany merely proves that the roots of prejudice run much deeper than intelligence or culture; they lie deep in the unchallenged thought processes of consciousness. Besides there's always a huge amount of mindless Samsara for the evil and the cunning to manipulate.

One could say that Hamsun's long held pro-German stance was legitimate anti-British anti-imperialism, one could say that his existentialism meant that he had no ideology at all or one could say that, in his 70s and 80s at the time, he had become a 'cantankerous old bugger'.

Still, perhaps the last word goes to the Norwegian lawyer who having read all of Hamsun's work and having found no trace of Nazism in it, when asked : ' How do you understand it ?' replied : 'I don't understand it'.

Marriage Home   Skogheim, Oppeid, Hamarøy

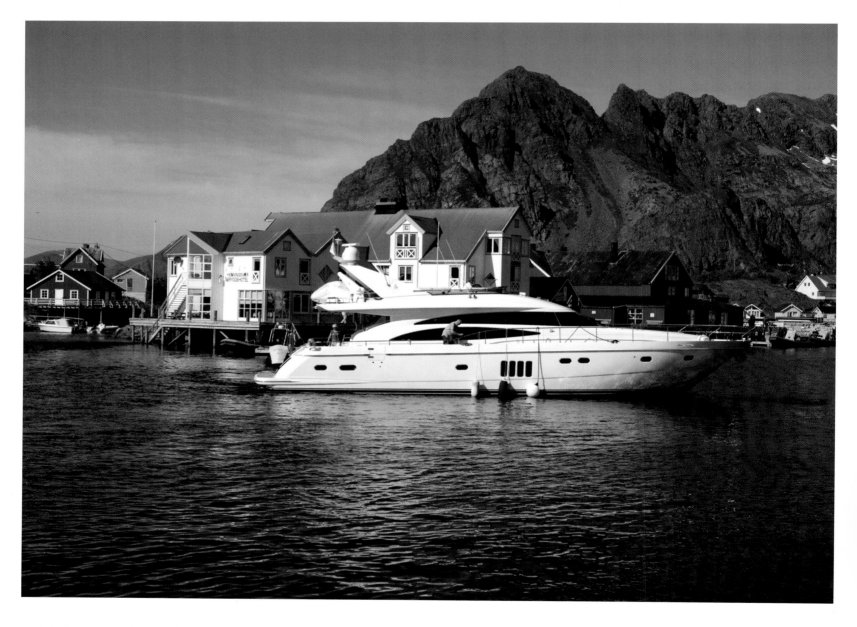

Majorstua Trawler   Henningsvaer, Lofoten   June 23

Majorstua is the trendy, fashion conscious, image obsessed district of Oslo

Summer Days   Sørvågen, Lofoten   June 22

Hen Party   Henningsvaer, Lofoten   June 23

The girl in the pink hat was to be married a few weeks later

The Right Place   Stamsund, Lofoten   June 23

To celebrate the midsummer and the realm of light, Norwegian families light fires and barbeqeues all along the coast.

This particular St Hansaften celebration had a special significance for Karl and Maria.

The beautiful Norwegian couple were to be married shortly afterwards in early August and had just received permission to build their house about 10-20 metres behind the camera

The above will be the view from their house when it is built

Midsummer Midnight Sun   Stamsund to Bødo   June 23

At 71'10" North, the North Cape is only 1,300 miles from the North Pole. With about half of the Arctic in terms of area, coastline, population and resources in Russian territory, Russia will dominate whatever happens to the Arctic environment as the Polar ice cap recedes. As the Northern Sea Route cuts the distance between W.Europe and the Far East by a third, it has already pushed very hard to open up commercial shipping lanes over Northern Russia during the Arctic Summer. Just four ships made the passage in 2010, but that increased to 34 in 2011, including oil tankers, fish factories and cruise liners. Soon to be permanently based in Tromsø in Northern Norway, the Arctic Council appears to be working well between the various Arctic nations and, for the time being, Russia adopts a co-operative strategy at its meetings.

The Arctic   Noordkaap, Magerøy   June 27

Journey's End   Noordkaap, Magerøy   June 27

Musician, Teacher, Craftsman   Kjell Åtle Sagen, Honningsvåg, Magerøy   June 27

From Kjell and Mona's House   Honningsvåg, Magerøy   June 27

Meet Me At The Grand Cafe   Karl Johans Gate, Oslo   June 28

'Talking Of Young Days'   Grand Cafe, Oslo   June 28

At the start of World War II, Marie Eggen (left) and Anne Sofie Sörli were both entering
their teens in Elverum to the North East of Oslo.

Elverum served as a temporary capital of Norway during the invasion by Nazi Germany.
On 9 April 1940 Norwegian troops prevented German parachute troops from capturing
Norway's King Haakon VI, Crown Prince, and Parliament while the Parliament was
meeting to issue the Elverum Authorization, which authorized the exiled government
until the Parliament could convene again. Two days later, shortly after the government's
refusal to submit to German terms, the center of Elverum was reduced to ashes. The
occupation by Nazi Germany is still a vivid memory and its termination is marked each
year on May 8th - Liberation Day, a flag flying day though not a public holiday.

In spite of such horrific circumstances, Marie and Anne Sofie were still young girls
bursting with life. They found solace and companionship deep in the mountains and
forests and, in their own words, 'had much fun'.

So that he could pick up from where he left off after lunch, Henrik Ibsen would put down his pen in the middle of a sentence, and take his daily stroll down Karl Johans Gate to the Grand Café to meet with some of the most famous writers, artists, academics and diplomats of the day. It was said that one could set one's watch by Ibsen's walk.

The restaurant opened in 1874, and quickly became a favoured venue for the capital's literati, evident in the 1928 mural at one end of the dining room which portrays many of the café's famous habitués of the 1890s. There is a real sense of history about the Grand Café, one can still sit more or less where Ibsen sat each day and the wood-panelled interior and smart brass fittings are much as they were when Ibsen ate his lunch of an open sandwich, a beer and a schnapps.

Today, the Grand Café is a breakfast restaurant, a hectic and a busy lunch venue for business people, and an "in" place in the evening. It is both popular and elegant at the same time.

In The Footsteps Of Ibsen   Grand Cafe, Oslo   June 28

National Theatre   Karl Johans Gate, Oslo   June 29

Torvald : ' Nobody sacrifices his honour for the one he loves'

Nora : ' Hundreds and thousands of women have'

Outside the Hotel Luna in Amalfi, near Naples, a plaque reads 'Casa di Bambola - Henrik Ibsen.'
The man who had said to understand me you must know Norway, spent almost all the twenty eight
years from 1864-1891 outside Norway. 'A Doll's House' / 'Casa di Bambola', 'Brand', 'Perr Gynt' ,
'Ghosts', and 'Wild Duck' were all written in Italy; 'League of Youth' , 'Enemy of the People', 'Pillars of
Society', 'Rosmershom', 'Lady from the Sea' and 'Hedda Gabler' in Germany. Controversy, alcoholism,
bankruptcy and scandal followed him every step of the way. 'Ghosts' was first performed in Chicago
in 1882 after causing a furore in Europe. It's amazing he got through it all.

'Master Builder', 'Little Eyolf', 'John Gabriel Borkman' and 'When The Dead Awaken' came from his
sojourn at a rather grand apartment near the King's Palace in Kristiana (Oslo) from 1891 onwards.
His son, a prominent polititian, married the daughter of Bjornsterne Bjornson, the Nobel Laureate
and showman intellectual of the day as Ibsen himself gradually became a pillar of society.

But perhaps most tellingly, was his reputation for continually changing his point of view and for
contradicting whatever was being said or he had said previously. Was this aversion to fixed positions the
secret formula that enabled him to enter the different realities of the characters that inhabit his plays ?
It's tempting to think so, not least because of Ibsen's last words on his deathbed : ' .....on the contrary....'

Nora : ' I believe that first and foremost I am an individual, just as much as you are'

181

So Long Marianne

Through the power of his writing and through the beauty of his songs, one of the most well know love affairs of the 1960's was that between Leonard Cohen, the Canadian poet-singer-songwriter, and the Norwegian model and muse, Marianne Jensen/Ihlen, who met on the Greek Island of Hydra. As Leonard later described it :

' And then I started to bump into these wonderful people, like Marianne and her husband, the Norwegian writer, Axel Jensen.......both the Greek and the foreigner had the feeling of the people that I was meant to be with. It was a great sense of inevitability and hospitality.....

I remember seeing Marianne with Axel and with the baby and thinking "what a beautiful holy trinity they are".. they were all blond and beautiful and suntanned. I saw Marianne several times before she saw me, but I do remember bumping into her at Catsicus, the grocery store.

(Marianne's biographer : ' Axel had left the island. Marianne and their little six month old son for another woman...... one day Marianne was in the village shop with her basket waiting to pick up bottled water and milk and a dark man stood in the doorway with the sun behind him. He said: "Would you like to join us, we're sitting outside?" It was Leonard Cohen. He called her the most beautiful woman he had ever met.')

'Oh, Marianne was terrific, and of course at that age one is mostly interested in beauty.... and she had beauty in abundance....and then she was an old-fashioned girl, and I kind of come from an old-fashioned background myself..... things that I took for granted with Marianne, and she perhaps took with me, a certain kind of courtesy and behaviour and ritual and order.... the house was very orderly and there was always a gardenia on my desk where I'd work...

There wasn't a man that wasn't interested in Marianne, there was no one that wasn't interested in approaching that beauty and that generosity..... it wasn't just that she was a traditional Nordic beauty, that was indisputable, but she was also very kind, and she was one of the most modest people about her beauty.

There was no sense that she was playing her beauty, or maybe she was so brilliant at it that no one saw. But you meet people, men and women, that are aware of their physical and use it, but with Marianne one felt a real modesty, that she was unaware of how good she looked.

She was brought up by her grandmother in Larkollen during the war ...and the grandmother was obviously in touch with a more ancient world. So Marianne inherited this very ancient sense of service and generosity, and it was totally natural, it was in the skin...just the way she put the plate on the table or poured the wine or...

Yes, we drove from Athens to Oslo in her little Carmen Gia, and she liked to drive fast, and I didn't like to drive that fast, but anyway, we got there. That was a wonderful drive. I don't know whether it was about the driving or not, but I do remember us quarreling a lot. But they were healed because we'd stop at some little Italian cafe and have pasta and a bottle of wine or some cheese and bread, and we' d get over it. But I remember coming in to Oslo......and another time by train, from Yugoslavia, and my coat was stolen in the train, and I got into Oslo in the middle of a snowstorm without a coat.......

Oslo, that's a city I really like .....for someone who studied literature at university, to come to Oslo and go to the national theatre and see Ibsen, that was incredible..... something about the scale in Oslo that is very similar to Montreal, just the space, the buildings...the snow falling...

And Norway has always been, curiously enough,......very hospitable to my work... that was not common... that didn't happen in every country, but it happened to an unusual degree in Norway, and I always had a curious connection with Norway in my life. So somehow my relationship with Scandinavia, Norway in particular, somehow that experience was… my experience was affirmed in Norway. I don't really understand how that happened, but it did '

'Those relationships at that time were all doomed, we didn't know it at the time that they were doomed, but ... those relationships that were formed idealistically or sexually or romantically couldn't survive what life imposed on us, the challenges that ordinary lives would confront them with. So none of those relationships survived, except in the sense that we honour them, and we recognize the nourishment of those experiences.'

Marianne : ' Oh, those years were really good. Very good. We sat in the sun and we lay in the sun, we walked in the sun, we listened to music, we bathed, we played, we drank, we discussed. There was writing and lovemaking and... It was absolutely fabulous, you know, to have it like that. During five years I didn't have shoes on my feet... sure, sure, in the wintertime I had something on my feet...... And I met many beautiful people..... Now they are cast to the winds. Some are dead.......many are dead..........'

During his triumphant return to the world stage in 2008, before playing 'Take This Waltz' at the end of the concert in Oslo, Leonard made the following dedication :

' I want to dedicate this last song to an old friend of mine, who passed away a few years ago, the great Norwegian writer, Axel Jensen...he was married to Marianne.....it was through these two wonderful people that I became introduced to your great country'

Separation   Edvard Munch   1896

'I loved you in the morning, our kisses deep and warm
Your hair upon the pillow like a sleepy golden storm'

Leonard Cohen 1967

Oil on canvas, 96.5 x 127 cm, Munch Museum, Oslo, MM M 24 Woll M 393

The Human   Vigeland Sculpture Park, Oslo   June 28

Integral   Vigeland Sculpture Park, Oslo   June 28

Empathy   Vigeland Sculpture Park, Oslo   June 28

Girlhood   Vigeland Sculpture Park, Oslo   June 28

Manhood   Vigeland Sculpture Park, Oslo   June 28

The Ring   Vigeland Sculpture Park, Oslo   June 28

seven billion

100,000 seconds = 27.8 hours   1 million seconds = 11.6 days   1 billion seconds = 31.7 years

The difference between a stadium crowd of 100,000 people and the total population of the world
is the same as the difference between 28 hours and 222 years

Tiruvannamalai   6,985,119,415   January

Mexico City   6,992,560,207   February

Saigon   **7,000,000,000**   March 12th

Rome   7,004,992,085   April

Chicago   7,011,237,024   May

Oslo   7,017,543,964   June

Singapore   7,024,140,935   July

Sydney   7,030,737,906   August

Paris   7,037,122,072   September

Tunis   7,043,719,043   October

Accra   7,050,103,209   November

Buenos Aires   7,056,700,180   December

Sujud   Masjid Agung, Yogyakarta   July 27

indonesia   july

Qiyaam   Masjid Agung, Yogyakarta   July 27

Ruku   Masjid Agung, Yogyakarta   July 27

Sujud   - 'Subhana Rabbiyal A'ala' / 'Glory be to God, the Most High'. Recited three times.
          (previous page)

Qiyaam - The first chaper of the Koran is recited in Arabic :
          'In the name of God (Allah), the compassionate, the merciful........ '

Ruku   - 'Subhana rabbiyal adheem' / 'Glory be to God, the Most Great'. Recited three times.

Great Mosque   Masjid Agung, Yogyakarta   July 27

Though known of from early on in the Islamic era through traveling Indian and Arab spice merchants
and through the Malaccan Sultanate, it was only from the 14th century onwards that Islam in Indonesia
began to spread peacefully, fragmentarily, over a long period of time and in harmony with other faiths
and indigenous cultures; Islam did not exist outside of Sumatra and Java before the 16th century. Under
the banner of non-orthodox 'Javanese Islam', Indonesia developed a more relaxed, polyglot spiritual
culture of its own, well away from the monolithic centralism and hard edged devotion of other branches
of the faith. The Masjid Agung / Great Mosque of Yogyakarta, built in 1773, is noted for its traditional
Javanese style of architecture.

Durian And Rickshaw   Jalan Malioboro, Yogyakarta   July 27

Once Upon A Time In Indonesia   Borobudur Temple, Java   July 27

Extraordinary and inspirational Buddhist and Hindu temples, built over many centuries, dignify and elevate the cultural history of Asia. The Buddhist Temple of Borobudur forms part of a great heritage that stretches from the Buddhist cities of Pagan in Burma, Anuradhupura and Polonnaruwa in Sri Lanka through to the awesome Hindu sites of Chidambaram and Brihadeeswara in Tamil Nadu, Angkor Wat in Cambodia and Prambanam in nearby Yogyakarta.

Upon seeing a medieval church in Europe, it is quite natural to wonder what life must have been like under such a Christian firmament. Even though Samsara is always a limiting factor, with the great temples of Asia, it is hard not to imagine what daily life must have felt like in societies where meditation and spiritual practice would have been present and widespread.

Meditating World   Borobudur Temple, Java   July 27

A Mahayana Buddhist Temple and pilgrimage site built during the 9th century Saliendra dynasty, Borobudur consists of a mandala shaped stepped pyramid structure, 120 metres square at the base supporting six square terraces, rising to three circular platforms, topped by a large central stupa surrounded by 72 buddha statues meditating in small latticed bell shaped stupas.

The pilgrim begins at the base of the monument, passing by over 1,400 narrative relief panels, in the process ascending through three layers - through the world of desires, the world of forms and through the world of formlessness. At that point, the realm of Samadhi begins to beckon, Samadhi (Sama : Equal / Dhi : Mind) is the state of consciousness whereby one looks at all phenomena with an equal mind.

Some would say that this is the actual nature of consciousness itself.

Meditating Buddhas   Borobudur Temple, Java   July 27

Temple Dancers   Borobudur Temple, Java   July 27

1,200 Years Later   Banjar Lebah, Denpasar, Bali   July 26

The structure of Balinese society is built around the banjar, a small village, a hamlet or a community of 200 or so households. It is made up of adult men who must be married and have a female partner – a wife, sister, mother or daughter. While the men deal with the administration of the banjar, the women attend to its cultural life.

As the banjar owns the property that lies between houses, the streets and ditches, and public buildings including the village hall, the members of the banjar`are responsible for roads and buildings, security, preparing food for ceremonies, building ritual structures for cremations, settling disputes and ensuring compliance with the village rules. The banjar members meet every 35 days. If a member is not able to be present they are required to pay a fine. Once a man's sons have become adults and married, the father can retire from his banjar responsibilities. If a person in the banjar dies without an heir their property is transferred to the banjar. Until recently only sons could inherit their father's property. In 2010 the law was changed allowing daughters to inherit a portion of her father's land if there are no sons.

Fan Dance   Banjar Lebah, Denpasar, Bali   July 26

As a child in the 1940s, Ni Ketut Arini helped her parents work in the fields whilst studying dance from ten years old at the village hall. Her fascination with dance led to dance school, teacher's training college and then travelling the world with Balinese dance.

Now in her late 60s, if she could get one wish, it would be, "as long as I remain with years, I can always teach and make people good at dancing." "I've never been bored of dancing. There is happiness in the heart when I make people happy with the dance that I offer them."

Legong Class   Ni Ketut Arini, Banjar Lebah, Denpasar, Bali   July 26

Legong   Balerung Mandera, Peliatan, Bali   July 31

With demanding technique requiring extreme suppleness of the body and traditionally performed by girls who have not yet reached puberty, Legong dancers begin rigorous official training anything from the age of five. In the womb they are played Balinese music and as soon as they are born, they learn the craft from their mothers, being taught to dance with their hands before they can walk. Performed by sumptuously costumed girls crowned with frangipanis, Legong is characterised by highly stylised slow movements, its delicacy being heightened by the young age of the performers, many of whom retire at the tender age of 18. Legong dancers are regarded highly in the society and often become wives of royal personages or wealthy merchants.

Tourism has increased the general level of wealth so that many banjar can now afford two or three different kinds of gamelan and support a greater variety of music and dance, but tourism has taken its toll on the traditions. Rather than prepubescent girls, young even mature women now perform and the dramas have been severely cut : 'The shorter dances for tourists are not true Balinese culture. The movements are the same but the dances are not complete.' Fortunately, the passion for dancing continues to burn in Balinese girls to this day : 'It is an embarrassment for any girl from Peliatan not to dance. Everyone here must dance.' Only the most talented and charismatic few will eventually graduate to perform in public. They are the future and life of the legong dance.

Drama   Balerung Mandera, Peliatan, Bali   July 31

Ritual   Balerung Mandera, Peliatan, Bali   July 31

Gamelan   Balerung Mandera, Peliatan, Bali   July 31

Frangipani   Balerung Mandera, Peliatan, Bali   July 31

Baris Dance   Balerung Mandera, Peliatan, Bali   July 31

Warrior   Balerung Mandera, Peliatan, Bali   July 31

Performed by young Balinese men, the Baris dance enacts the rite de passage from boyhood to manhood.
Originally performed as a religious ritual in order to dedicate soldiers and their weapons, it depicts
the feelings of the young warrior prior to battle.

Beautiful Bali   Town Centre, Kuta, Bali   July 29

Tranquil Ubud   Main Street, Ubud, Bali   July 31

Workmanship   Market Buildings, Ubud, Bali   July 31

Artistry   Central Bali   July 31

Subak are the irrigation societies that are responsible for ensuring that all the water in the irrigation system that feeds the rice fields is distributed fairly across the island. These associations were founded more than 1,000 years ago with the first reference to them in 1022. There are around 1,300 subak organisations across Bali with each one having about 200 members. Everyone who owns land must be a member of their subak and pay membership fees, and everyone within the subak organisation is equal, regardless of their caste. Everyone who is a member must attend monthly meetings and together they will decide about when rice will be planted and harvested, when to make offerings, how dams and ditches will be repaired, and what fertilizers or pesticides are to be used.

Subak   Ubud Area, Bali   July 31

Offerings   Countryside, Ubud, Bali   July 31

Coconut   Countryside, Ubud, Bali   July 31

Sate   Countryside, Ubud, Bali   July 31

Dedication   Countryside, Ubud, Bali   July 31

Blessing   Market Shrine, Ubud, Bali   July 30

Sacrament   Market Shrine, Ubud, Bali   July 31

Pilgrimage   Mother Temple, Besakih, Bali   July 31

Community   Mother Temple, Besakih, Bali   July 31

Sanctification   Mother Temple, Besakih, Bali   July 31

Return   Mother Temple, Besakih, Bali   July 31

227

Touching The Earth   Iron Knob, South Australia   Aug 03

australia   august

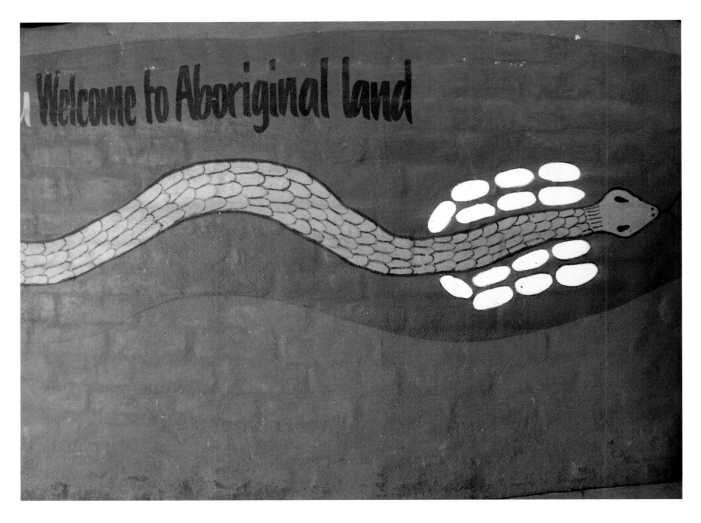

Serpent Being   Uluru, Northern Territory   Aug 07

Songlines   Airport, Alice Springs, Northern Territory   Aug 05

Red   Uluru, Northern Territory   Aug 05

Ancestral Beings   Kata Tjuta, Northern Territory   Aug 06

The world was once a featureless place. None of the places we know existed until creator beings, in the forms of people, plants and animals, traveled widely across the land.

Then, in a process of creation and destruction, they formed the landscape as we know it today. Anangu land is still inhabited by the spirits of dozens of 'Tjukuritja' or 'Waparitja', ancestral creator beings. (Anangu Myth)

Otherwise, the mythology surrounding Kata Tjuta is mostly not disclosed to outsiders. Many ceremonies were, and still are, carried out there, particularly at night

Dreamtime   Uluru, Northern Territory   Aug 05

Every person exists eternally in the Dreaming. This eternal part existed before the life of the individual begins and continues to exist when the life of the individual ends. Before and after life, it is believed that the spirit-child exists in the Dreaming and is only initiated into life by being born through a mother. The spirit of the child enters the developing fetus during the fifth month of pregnancy, when the mother feels the child first move in the womb

In the Aboriginal world view, every event leaves a record in the land. Everything in the natural world is a result of the past, present and future actions of the archetypal beings, whose actions are continuously creating the world. Whilst Europeans consider these cultural ancestors to be mythical, many Aboriginal people believe in their present and future literal existence. The meaning and significance of particular places and creatures is wedded to their origin in the Dreaming, and certain places have a numinous potency, which the Aborigines call its 'dreaming'. In this dreaming resides the sacredness of the earth.

Extraction   Iron Knob, South Australia   Aug 03

Employment   Iron Knob, South Australia   Aug 03

Iron Red   Iron Knob, South Australia   Aug 03

In the Royal Bank of Australia's 'Overview' report of February 2013, after various introductory comments about the world economy, the first factors it looked at were the prices of iron ore and coal. In May 2012, the Bank reported : ' Iron ore is Australia's most significant export, accounting for around 20 per cent of total export values in 2011 - 70 per cent of the iron ore exports are destined for China... most of the remaining 30 per cent.... to Japan and Korea'. That is, the motor cars and bicycles, the washing machines and ipads that we buy in the West are dug out of the ground in places like Western Australia. W Australia likes to boast that it is the saviour of the Australian economy; probably overstated but the resources boom is definitely what has kept the wolf from the door of every Australian citizen during the current world economic crisis.

Hancock Prospecting   Ventnoor Avenue, West Perth, Western Australia   Aug 02

The World's Wealthiest Woman

With a strident, ruthless, dogmatic, partisan 'in-your-face-here-I-am' single minded attitude, Gina Hancock Rinehart is a classic Australian story. No amount of quibbling about inherited wealth, no amount of sniping about family relationships should in any way detract from the fact that her success in turning around a failing family enterprise into a giant of world mining is a phenomenal achievement, worthy of the utmost respect.

The story famously starts in the early 1950s with her father, Lang Hancock, being forced to reroute his light aircraft to avoid bad weather in the Pilbara in Western Australia and realising that the landscape he was flying through was planet iron : ' On going through a gorge in the Turner River, I noticed that the walls looked to me to be solid iron and was particularly alerted by the rusty looking colour of it, it showed it to me to be oxidised iron' Hancock returned to the area many times and, accompanied by prospector Ken McCamey, followed the iron ore over a distance of 112 km. He soon came to realise that he had stumbled across reserves of iron ore so vast that they could supply the entire world.

It took Hancock another ten years to obtain the mining concessions and leases to 500 square kilometres of the Pilbara, eventually leading to a joint venture with Rio Tinto, netting him $10 mn US in annual royalties and making Lang Hancock a very wealthy man.

On his death in 1993, the business was heavily in debt but the key assets, the royalties on the leases, were transferred to Gina, by that time a widow and a mother of four. Brought up as Lang Hancock's 'right hand man' and as his nominated successor. Gina had dropped out of college to start working for her father and had gained an immense knowledge of the Pilbara iron ire industry.

Lang Hancock concentrated on exploration and accumulating vast mining leases but Gina focused on developing Hancock Prospecting's undeveloped deposits, raising capital through joint venture partnerships and turning the leases into revenue creating productive mines.

Via Hancock Prospecting, she shares 50 per cent of the profits generated by the 30 mn tonnes pa joint venture with Rio Tinto, and her new Roy Hill iron ore project, also in the Pilbara, is expected to produce 55 mn tonnes pa from 2013 onwards. There are further significant mining interests in manganese in the Pilbara and coal in Central Queensland.

The net result of all this is that Gina has increased her original family inheritance by about four hundred times, to the point where she is Australia's wealthiest person. Depending on the ups and downs of stockmarkets and exchange rates, she vies with Lillian Bettencourt, the L'Oreal heiress, in Paris, and the Walmart heiresses Christy and Alice Walton, to be the world's wealthiest woman. This being the case, one can straightaway conclude that of these four, Gina is the real deal, the real wealth creator - she's the one that's really doing it.

A person like Gina takes the gender debate to new areas. Not only is she one of a new breed of billionaire businesswomen, but her circumstance begins to isolate the issues underlying traditional male behaviour - what attributable to gender and what to being in traditional positions of power and authority ? It is becoming increasingly clear that successful women run up against exactly the same issues that men have traditionally borne - the burden of office in its various guises. One might tentatively suggest : ' Render unto Gender the things that are Gender's and unto Power the things that are Power's.'

And Gina has also kept the gossip columnists and social critics busy with her family bust-ups over control of the Hancock Trust's assets. Notwithstanding the vested interests of other members of the family, the Trust owns 24% of Hancock Prospecting, a mighty going concern and, as long as she is moving and shaking as she is, one can well understand why Gina, and many sensible Australians, would want Gina to remain its sole Trustee.

Amy Stewart   Mining Engineering Student   Adelaide

Queen Victoria Building   George Street, Sydney, New South Wales   Aug 08

Sydney Harbour   Sydney, New South Wales   Aug 08

Town Planner   Stephen Beattie, N Sydney, New South Wales   Aug 08

Million Dollar Plus Bungalows   Ridge Street, N Sydney, New South Wales   Aug 08

Sweet Innocent Things   St Leonard's Park, N Sydney, New South Wales   Aug 08

Where Did It All Go Wrong?   Tweed Valley Rollers, Gladstone, Queensland   Aug 11

Social Sport   Lions AFL Club, Brisbane, Queensland   Aug 11

Brisbane Scarlett   Lions AFL Club, Brisbane, Queensland   Aug 11

The World And Sport

XXX Olympiad - London, August 2012

Australia was one of the first countries to professionalize its sporting culture and to place success in sport as a central social objective. In all the disciplines from the 1950s onwards the nation had become accustomed to outstanding levels of sporting success, way out of proportion to the size of its population. In the preceding four Olympiads, Australia had amassed impressive medal hauls, placing it 7th, 4th, 4th and 6th in the medals tables. Sporting achievement had become a matter of great national pride.

Hanging By A Fingertip

As Australia entered the XXX Olympiad in London, its sporting prowess was already beginning to show large cracks. No male tennis players in the top 20 for five years, the once all conquering cricket team sliding down the world rankings and Cadel Evans, the 2011 Tour de France winner, slipping away to finish seventh. Aussie sports men and women were renowned for their mental toughness under pressure so, a month before the Olympics, the nation watched aghast as Adam Scott blew a four shot lead at the 15th hole to gift The Open title to Ernie Els.

The swimming events take place in the first few days of an Olympics and as Australia is traditionally very strong in swimming, what normally happens is that Australia goes right to the top of the medals table, rides high and slowly filters downwards during the rest of the Olympics. All was going to plan when the Aussie girls won the 4 x 100 mtrs freestyle relay on the first evening. Some question marks arose when the much fancied men's 4 x 100 mtrs freestyle relay team finished out of the medals the following day, but all eyes were on swimming's blue riband event, the men's 100 mtrs freestyle final, with the reigning world champion, James 'The Missile' Magnussen, a 6'5" specimen from Port Macquarrie, New South Wales. Slightly behind at the turn, Magnussen surged down the final length and five metres out. was a short head in front of the American, Nathan Adrian. Adrian charged the last five metres beating Magnussen to the touch by a hundredth of a second - literally a fingertip.

Although Magnussen's time (47.53) was faster than his world title winning time (47.63), he had been so hyped up beforehand, that the national disappointment was huge. Had Magnussen's fingertip made that touch, one suspects that Australia's Olympic journey would have been completely different, but much worse was to follow.

The swimming team continued to under-perform with no further golds and a ten medal haul, as opposed to the six golds and twenty medals in Beijing. In fact, Australia did not win another gold medal of any kind for the following few days at which point, by Day 9, it lay 24th in the medals table. It was a national sporting disaster.

Nation Overboard

What made it even more excruciating was that Australia's traditional sporting rival, Britain / England, was collecting yellow discs like cookies off a shelf, delighting in its most successful Olympics of the modern era. The 'm'aider' signal went out and was picked up by an unlikely source, the nation's yachtsmen, who threw out the national lifebelt and rescued three gold medals in the latter stages of the games. A modicum of respectability was restored to the nation's wounded pride by finishing tenth in the medals table, with seven golds, thirty five medals in all and ranking London 2012 in 11th position in Australia's 17 Olympiad's since 1948.

It had been a rough ride, the swimming team took the brunt of the criticism with rumours of sexual impropriety, doping, poor leadership etc, as one would expect in the various post-mortems. Massive commercial sponsorship intruded upon Australia's athletes, betting on their success in a very big way and maybe the athletes started believing their own advertising hype. Whatever, the recriminations will go all the way to the next Olympics in Rio de Janiero. As Australia's sporting foes know only too well, there's nothing so mean as a wounded Aussie. So watch out the rest of the world in 2016 !

Olympic Stadium   Sydney 2000

Aussie Green   Countryside, Port Wakefield, South Australia   Aug 04

Aussie Gold   Countryside, Port Wakefield, South Australia   Aug 04

Dirt Road   Countryside, Port Wakefield, South Australia   Aug 04

Souls   Pitt Street, Sydney, New South Wales   Aug 08

One could be forgiven for passing by the pharnacy at 160 Pitt Street in Sydney and thinking it a rather quaint building under a preservation order. There is nothing to suggest the massive 4 billion dollar industrial conglomerate that is headquartered there.

In 1872, Caleb Soul and his son Washington opened their first pharmacy on Pitt Street, Sydney, eventually relocating to 158-160. After hearing of Soul's success, Lewy Pattinson emigrated to Australia in 1881 and became good friends with Soul. They were never in competition in business, and in the early 1900s, the Souls asked Pattinson to buy their business. As a result, Pattinson and Co. bought out Washington H. Soul and Co. and out of respect for their friendship, the resultant entity became known as Washington H. Soul Pattinson and Company Limited. (WHSP) The first public offering of shares was in December 1902, and the company listed on the Sydney Stock Exchange in January 1903.

WHSP celebrated one hundred years as a public company in 2002 and is Australia's second-oldest listed company. Its headquarters remain at 160 Pitt Street Mall, Sydney and it is affectionately known as 'Souls' in financial markets after its stock market code 'SOL' - hardly surprising since 'Souls' has never failed to pay an annual dividend. Tbe present Chairman, Robert Milner, is Lewy Pattinson's great grandson.

Variously valued in recent years at A\$3.7-3.9 billion, WHSP is a diversified investor in building products, property, coal, telecommunications, rural services, pharmaceuticals, investment vehicles and a substantial portfolio of shares. Its interests include majority ownership of the New Acland coal mine (opposite) and the Queensland Bulk Handling coal export terminal at the Port of Brisbane (centre pic next page).

Currently, the mine is a major economic contributor to the region, providing a $300 million injection annually into SE Queensland's economy and $110 million each year to the Darling Downs. Hundreds of livelihoods depend on New Acland and have done for a decade. The operation employs more than 300 local people directly, and provides a further 160 full-time contractor jobs and 2,300 indirect jobs. Stage 3 of the development, subject to planning approval, proposes that current employment and economic benefits will not be lost to the Darling Downs. New Acland exports c. 65% of its thermal coal to niche markets in the Asia Pacific, incl. Japan, Korea and Chile.

New Acland Mine   Acland, Toowoomba, Queensland   Aug 10

Truck Love   Port Of Brisbane, Queensland   Aug 10

Old Acland Mine   Acland, Toowoomba, Queensland   Aug 10

Mining Hotel   Campbell Street, Oakey, Queensland   Aug 10

252

The World And Coal

World Coal Production MT (mn tons)			CO2 Emissions -		kg/GJ	CO2 Atmospheric -		ppm
1860	-	130	Natural Gas	-	75	pre 1850	-	275-285
1900	-	1,000	LPG	-	90	1900	-	300
1950	-	2,500	Oil	-	97	1950	-	320
1975	-	3,250	Coal	-	134	1975	-	330
2000	-	4,600	Electricity	-	150	2000	-	365
2010	-	7,200				2010	-	380

With the decline of coal mining and the rise of cleaner forms of energy, many in the West thought that coal based pollution was becoming a thing of the past. As the statistics above demonstrate, nothing could be further from the truth. Coal usage has rocketed in the last 25 years and has been the world's fastest-growing fuel in the past decade. Demand has grown at nearly twice the rate of natural gas and hydro power, and more than four times faster than global oil consumption. It is also expected to grow faster than other fuels in coming decades. This is not good news for the Earth's atmosphere.

This is almost wholly attributable to its increased usage in Asia where coal production doubled between 1980 and 2000, and more than doubled again between 2001 and 2010. China's share of world coal production increased from 16% to 44% and is now twice the demand for oil in the United States, and four times Saudi Arabia's production of oil. On top of that, in 2011, China became the world's largest importer of coal. The net result is that from 2000-10, the world pumped 100 billion tonnes of carbon into the atmosphere, about a quarter of all carbon dioxide put there by humanity since 1750.

Partly due to the autonomous economic development of the Asian economies, but mainly caused by the massive transfer of world manufacturing capacity to the Asia-Pacific, Western consumer goods previously produced under reasonable environmental regimes were transferred to countries with precious few environmental regulations. The Western consumer gorged themselves on twenty five years of cheap Asian products, ignoring the environmental damage being caused, not to mention the 'slave labour', as one Australian Trade Unionist put it.

Climate Science Change?

Just when climate change science should be delivering sun, sea and sex package tours to Greenland, the earth's atmosphere has done a runner. In what amounts to a doctrinal 'own goal' for climate change, the projected rise in the Earth's temperatures has simply not happened. Despite all the above statistics, global air temperatures have been flat for the last 15 years. Climate change sceptics will doubtless be rubbing their hands, but not due to the cold. Global air temperatures have risen by 1C in the last 100 years.

Europe To The Back Of The Class

The shale gas bonanza in the United States and Gazprom's screwing of the European gas market means that gas is three times as expensive in Europe as in the US. At the same time, the US coal industry 'dumped' millions of tons of surplus coal on international markets with the result that in November 2012, German utilities lost E11.70 per megawatt when they burned gas and earned E14.20 when they burned coal. In 2012 in the UK, coal based power generation was 50% higher than the previous year and overtook gas for the first time since 2007. This has made a nonsense of EU environmental policies and a mockery of Europe's sanctimonious 'greenier than thou' posturing.

Australia And Coal - 2011 - Total 414 MT, Export 284 MT (Japan 106.2 - Korea 45.7 - China 33.6)

Generating 75% of its electricity from coal but with substantial reserves and vast unexploited landscapes, Australia has responded to the changing world market, particularly now that China is importing coal. Exports will rise by an extra 200 MT by 2017 and huge new production facilities are coming on line to meet that demand. Coal accounts for 70% of the throughput of the Port of Gladstone (bottom left / top right), and its coal terminal is increasing its capacity from 30MTpa to 60 MTpa. Hancock Prospecting's A$7billion Alpha mine project in Central Queensland will eventually bring another 30MTpa on stream.

The China First Project - based on the purchase of 1.4 billion tons of coal mining rights in Central Queensland, with its offtake guaranteed by Chinese power generating companies and with 85% of its A$8billion cost underwritten by Chinese banks, China First is developing a 40MTpa facility that will open 6 mines, construct a 471km heavy goods railway and develop extensive port facilities at Abbot Point on the Queensland coast. With 10,000 people directly employed, 70,000 jobs indirectly created and with 10-15% Mining Royalties rolling in revenue for the State of Queensland, no-one is going to stop this kind of project.

253

Cranescape   Port of Gladstone, Queensland   Aug 11

Bauxite   Port of Gladstone, Queensland   Aug 11

Red Centre I   Kata Tjuta, Northern Territory   Aug 06

Red Centre II   William Street, Sydney, New South Wales   Aug 08

Eat   Drink   Love   La Palette, St Germain des Prés, Paris   Sept 08

'When I go back to England I have a subtle but persistent feeling of discomfort,
a constant moral pressure to think and say the right thing.'
The Secret Life of France, Lucy Wadham 2009

france   september

High Temple Of The Vine   Saint Émilion, Aquitaine   Sept 06

By Hand   Chateau Quercy, Vignonet, Aquitaine   Sept 05

Maze   Saint Émilion, Aquitaine   Sept 01

Chateau   Chateau Quercy, Vignonet, Aquitaine   Sept 05

Traditional   Chateau Quercy, Vignonet, Aquitaine   Sept 05

Trimming Saint Émilion, Aquitaine Sept 04

Grape Picker Chateau Beaurang, Saint Émilion, Aquitaine Sept 05

Fermentation   Chateau Beaurang, Saint Émilion, Aquitaine   Sept 05

Training   Saint Émilion, Aquitaine   Sept 05

Oak Barrelled   Chateau Mauvezin, Saint Émilion, Aquitaine   Sept 04

Olivier Cassat   Chateau Mauvezin, Saint Émilion, Aquitaine   Sept 04

Chateau Mauvezin,   Saint Émilion, Aquitaine   Sept 04

Wine Tasting   Ecole du Vin, Saint Émilion, Aquitaine   Sept 02

First Nose   Ecole du Vin, Saint Émilion, Aquitaine   Sept 02

Wine Merchant   Saint Émilion, Aquitaine   Sept 04

Caneles   Saint Émilion, Aquitaine   Sept 01

Bar Tabac   Saint Émilion, Aquitaine   Sept 05

Amelia Canta   Place d'Eglise, Saint Émilion, Aquitaine   Sept 05

Col du Tourmalet - 2115 m   Hautes Pyrénées   Sept 06

Queen Of The Mountains   Col d'Aubisque, Hautes Pyrénées   Sept 06

Col d'Aspin   Hautes Pyrénées   Sept 06

Va Va Voom   Col d'Aubisque, Hautes Pyrénées   Sept 06

Tour de France

Man Versus Machine - Stage 16, 2012 - Pau to Bagnères de Luchon

After the infuriating sabotage of Stage 14, when metal tacks were scattered amongst the riders causing numerous punctures, Stage 16 loomed large. Billed as the toughest of the 2012 Tour, it was the Stage favoured for attacks on the Tour Yellow Jersey, donned by Britain's Bradley Wiggins going into the race. As it turned out, Wiggins and his Sky team handled the counter attacks with relative ease and Stage 16 was the Stage which finally saw off the challenge of the previous year's Tour winner, the Australian Cadel Evans, who lost a title conceding 4mins 47secs to Wiggins.

The French cyclist, Thomas Voeckler won the Stage, as he described it in his post-race interview. "I've raced in these mountains since the age of 10.....I know every kilometre off by heart and I went through four passes today. It's only beginning to dawn on me now what I've achieved. Cycling's an obsession for me, but today feels like something to exceed them all.'

Voeckler had ridden 197 kilometres up and down over four precipitous mountain passes in a winning time of 5hrs 35mins 02 secs....... Hold on ! 197 Ks in 5:35 ? .... that immediately prompted the question: how much faster could it be done by car ? As it so happens, the camera is very used to being driven on mountain roads, knows how to handle them at fast but safe, sub-maniacal speeds and was intrigued to establish the answer to this question. The gauntlet had been thrown down, the challenge could not be resisted.

When a marathon runner completes a marathon in 2hrs 5mins, he has been running at 12.5 mph / 20 kph - speeds that most people would be pushed to bicycle at ! Inside your house, place a mark on a wall at 2.45 metres from the ground, stand a metre away and look up at the mark - what you are looking at is the world High Jump record set by the great Cuban athlete, Javier Sotomayor, in Salamanca in Spain in July 1993. Even more absurd, if you have a corridor long enough, is to place two marks 8.95 mtrs apart on a floor and what you are looking at is the world Long Jump record set in Tokyo in August 1991 by the leaping American, Mike Powell. Until we put these records into everyday contexts, we just don't realize the phenomenal achievements of the world's athletes.

The four Cols on Stage 16 - d'Aubisque, du Tourmalet, d'Aspin and de Peyresourde - are 1,709 mtrs, 2,115 mtrs, 1,489 mtrs and 1,509 mtrs high with ascents of 30.1 kms, 19 kms, 12.8 kms and 9.96 kms respectively - a tortuously steep ascent total of 61.8 kms. The mountain bends on the way up would be grueling enough but it is the 70-100 kph descents down crash barrier free precipitous mountain roads, something akin to continuous ski jumping, that definitively mark out such Tour riders as a special breed of men.

Mais naturellement, bien sur et de rigeur, un Va Va Voom auto francais was specifically hired for the task, fuelled up ready, pawing at the ground in Pau. Of course, the camera observed every speed limit (big wide innocent lens) and utilised its higher flat line and semi-rallying climbing expertise to maximum effect wherever possible. With four photo breaks totaling 31 mins, four excess congestion allowances totaling 21 mins and allowing another 5-10 mins for 'wrong routing' through various of the towns and villages, but otherwise driving Stage 16 full-on non-stop, the picture that emerged was that despite the huge mechanical advantage of the internal combustion engine over the human being going up hills and on open roads, the motor car was still not even twice as fast as Thomas Voeckler's 5 hrs 35 mins. The Va Va Voom took 3.00 hrs to 3hrs 05 mins to make it to Bagnères de Luchon.

As for the challenge, the camera found the ride 'interesting', especially those vertiginous scenic views vertically downwards from the edges of the mountain roads, but does not in general recommend the experience to others !

Col de Peyresourde   Hautes Pyrénées

La Grande Épicerie   St Germain des Prés, Paris   Sept 08

Fromage Verité   St Germain des Prés, Paris   Sept 08

Plat du Jour   Rue de Bellville, Belleville, Paris   Sept 10

Window Cuisine   La Marais, Paris   Sept 09

Rendezvous   La Palette, St Germain des Prés, Paris   Sept 08

La Nuit   La Palette, St Germain des Prés, Paris   Sept 08

Image I   Rue de Bellville, Belleville, Paris   Sept 04

Image II   Rue de Lille, Rive Gauche, Paris   Sept 09

The World And Wealth - Liberté   Égalité   Luxury

'Paris est un vrai trompe-l'œil, un superbe décor habité par quatre millions de silhouettes'
'Paris truly deceives the eye - a magnificent phoney setting inhabited by four million silhouettes'.
Albert Camus - La Chute / The Fall - 1956

As the permanent world capital of illusion, if there is anywhere to disport oneself in the world, it's Paris - it is a flaunter's paradise. As the culture of artifice has been honed to a fine degree over the centuries, Paris is ideally suited to 'do luxury'. It is the undisputed centre of the world's luxury goods industry, LVMH, Hermes, PPR, Chanel, Cartier dominate their sector. In the 2010s, luxury goods sales have surged ahead at double digit growth rates. With the western economies reeling from austerity, has the world completely lost its bearings? Or are the wealthy thumbing their noses at the poor and deprived, a 21st century globalised version of 'Let them eat cake'? This needs some explaining.

Equality - if this means material equality then, as all human beings are different, look at each other in different ways and possess different desires, drives and abilities in the material world, no such thing as equality exists in reality. Apart from a few isolated, idealistic communities, when has such social equality ever existed ? It is hard to argue with George Orwell : 'Inequality is the unalterable law of human life'. This being the case, the only way to establish material equality is to abolish private property, private possessions, personal wealth and all forms of money. All material requirements would then be supplied equally to everyone on a rations book basis. As The State would control the supply of goods, this power of the State would then be vested in certain individuals. As evidenced by the wealth of Party members and their families in numerous 'Communist' regimes, George Orwell's most famous law then applies ; 'All animals are equal, but some are more equal than others'.

Inequality - the surge in the luxury goods industry is based on one inescapable fact, there is more inequality in the world. Over the last 25 years, the world economy is bigger with greater overall wealth, it has been restructured by a huge technological revolution and that restructuring has transferred economic power and wealth from the more egalitarian parts of the world to the less equal parts of the world - from the West to Asia in short. Dubbed 'The Rise Of The Rest', Singapore is awash with hundreds of thousands of millionaires, China is accumulating male and female billionaires at jaw dropping rates.

The Redistributive Effect Of The State - United Kingdom. After a century of rising government expenditure and in the mid-range of taxation regimes, until 2010, the capitalisation of UK Gov at £1 trillion meant that every household in Britain owned about £25k-£30k of State assets. Unfortunately during the 2010s, the continuing rise in the National Debt will wipe this out. What therefore is the redistributive value of those State services provided on an annual basis - free Health, free Education, and the social safety net ?

About 12.5% of the UK population of 63 million opt for private health and private education. For the purpose of analysis, the remaining 55 million are separated into 35 million Middle Income, receiving free Education and Health, and 20 million Low Income, receiving social welfare in addition. Total government expenditure in 2012 is £568 bn - Health £121.3 bn / Education £91.7 bn / Welfare £116.1 bn. Therefore, 35 million Middle Income people receive approx. £3,400 worth of State services per annum per person and Low Income people receive an extra £5,800 of welfare, £9,200 per annum per person in total. The rest of State expenditure (£240 bn) is spread across all citizens at an extra £3,800 per person. Summary :
All Citizens - £3,800 pa , Middle Income - £7,200 pa, Low Income - £13,000 pa. So very, very broadly, a top rate taxpayer who pays £50k pa in all taxes receives £5,000 pa in benefits, and transfers £9,000 pa to five low income people. This is the redistributive effect of UK taxation.

The Triumph Of The Object - Anyone who has ever ridden in a Rolls Royce can attest to the sense of status that it confers. All things considered, it does a remarkably good job at deluding its occupants into thinking that they are superior beings. In actual fact, what has happened is that the luxury goods company has very profitably exploited the owner's need for status. One could argue that the purchase of status is based on a prior lack of self-esteem, on the need to express superior identity through an object. Greenie, left-wing, liberal lifestylers are no different, they have their own techie, eco, arty, cool range of thingamajigs that project their identities through their own discreet, stylised product mix.

The digital age has produced unparalleled powers of 'introjection' into the individual psyche and there is no more pure form of marketing than luxury brand marketing, the power to persuade a person to buy something for more than it's worth. One cannot help but conclude that the rise of the luxury goods industry signifies the triumph of materialism in general - whereby people increasingly project themselves and see others in terms of the objects they possess.

Love Me Serge   Rue de Lille, Rive Gauche, Paris   Sept 09

All Before Them   Rue de la Villette, Belleville, Paris   Sept 10

Metro   Paris   Sept 08

Metrosexual   Paris   Sept 08/09

White Light   Canal St Martin, Paris   Sept 09

La Famille   Canal St Martin, Paris   Sept 09

Sacred Heart   Sacré Coeur, Montmartre, Paris   Sept 09

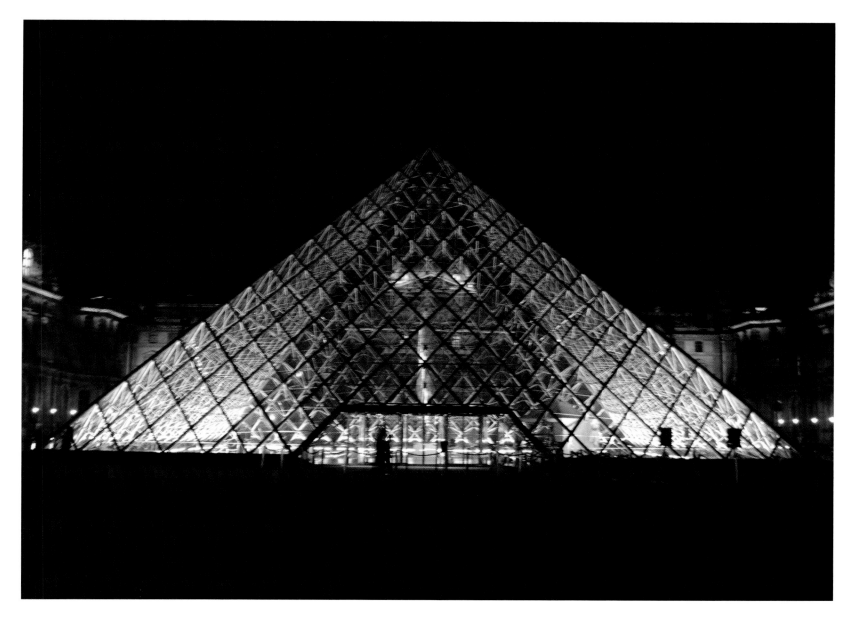

Object Image   Louvre, Paris   Sept 08

Minarets Old And New   Ouled Al Naceur, Gafsa   Oct 16

On December 17th, 2010 in Sidi Bouzid, a deprived, marginalised provincial town between Kerouan and Gafsa, a humble market trader, Mohamed Bouazizi, immolated himself outside the local governor's offices as a result of severe harassment and humiliation by local officials. Crowds gathered immediately to express their horror and anger. The protest was filmed on his mobile phone by Ali Al Bouazizi, a political analyst, edited with friends and uploaded to Facebook. It aired on Al Jazeera news, which was then picked up on satellite dishes all over Tunisia, which then went nationwide on mobile phones and Facebook.

The Arab awakening had begun.

tunisia   october

Sahara   Elfaouar, Douz   Oct 18

'The Arab Street?'   Bir El Hajla, Chott El Jerrid   Oct 18

Chott Oasis   Oued El Oudel, Chott Gharsa   Oct 17

Bonjour !   Oued El Oudel, Chott Gharsa   Oct 17

Datte First Class   Nefta, Tozeur   Oct 18

Date Pickers   Outskirts, Tozeur   Oct 18

Oasis   Nefta, Tozeur   Oct 18

Morning Market   Souk El Ahad, Kebili   Oct 18

Tribesmen   Douz, Kebili   Oct 18

Hustle And Bustle   Douz, Kebili   Oct 18

Food And Babies   Souk El Ahad, Kebili   Oct 18

Previously in the south, a traditional procession of an adorned camel, called the jehfa, accompanied by the tunes of flute and drums, used to carry the bride to her husband's home. The Chabbia area of Tozeur was one of the last places where a bride would ride on such a camel born litter at her marriage ceremony. Nowadays, this habit has disappeared - the jehfa still joins the procession but is now only used for decoration, with the bride either walking alongside the camel or going to her husband's by car. Weddings of southern Tunisian tribes are characterised by dishes such as couscous with lamb, horsemanship, bedouin songs, and the presence of traditional clothes.

Jehfa   Ave Farhat Hached, Tozeur   Oct 18

Wedding Sweets   Ave Ali Behouane, Kairouan   Oct 20

Wedding Guests   Ave Farhat Hached, Tozeur   Oct 18

Fertility   Boussalem, Jendouba   Oct 24

Olive Grove   Countryside, Sidi Bouzid   Oct 24

Shepherd   Countryside, Beja   Oct 24

Greens   Taboursouk, Beja   Oct 22

Grain   Essouassi, Mahdia   Oct 21

Livestock   Farmer's Market, Testour   Oct 22

Flatbreads   Ave Ali Behouane, Kairouan   Oct 20

Old Mosque   Medina, Kairouan   Oct 20

Mashrabiya Window   Ave Ali Behouane, Kairouan   Oct 20

Brewing   Cafe Sabra, Kairouan   Oct 20

Baking   Medina, Kairouan   Oct 20

Planing   Medina, Kairouan   Oct 20

Mixing   Medina, Kairouan   Oct 20

All The Rage   Headscarves, Ave Ali Behouane, Kairouan   Oct 20

Unveiled   Main Street, Nefza, Beja   Oct 24

Dignified   Main Street, Nefza, Beja   Oct 24

Old Times   Main Street, Nefza, Beja   Oct 24

You Say You Want A Revolution   Medina, Tunis   Oct 25

Adolescence   Rapped Up, Kairouan   Oct 19

Cafe El Habib   Nefta, Tozeur   Oct 17

Islamic Revolution   Ennahda Party Meeting, Place Des Martyrs, Kairouan   Oct 19

Rap Revolution   Place Des Martyrs, Kairouan   Oct 20

Straight Onto Facebook   Cultural Centre, Kairouan   Oct 19

Rapper   Cultural Centre, Kairouan   Oct 19

Rap Event   Cultural Centre, Kairouan   Oct 19

The Tunisian Exception

During the 2000s and under the auspices of the United Nations Development Programme, a group of Arab intellectuals and scholars subjected the state of the Arab world to a rigorous examination. The UN Arab Human Development Reports - 2002-2009 - were downloaded in their millions and were described as the most widely read publications in Arabic since the Koran. In addressing the questions : 'What has gone wrong with the Arab world ?' 'Why is it stuck so far behind the times ?', the original report identified three major 'deficits' that afflicted the 22 countries that make up the Arab League : The Freedom Deficit, The Knowledge Deficit.and The Gender Deficit.

Freedom Deficit - Despite the outward trappings of Democracy, in the UNDP's view, the lack of basic freedoms hold much of the Arab world back - the survival of absolute autocracies, the holding of bogus elections, confusion between the executive and the judiciary (closely linked linguistically in Arabic), constraints on the media and on civil society; and a patriarchal, intolerant, sometimes suffocating social environment. Not surprisingly, large sections of Arab youth are said to want to get out as fast as they can.

Knowledge Deficit - Since the heyday of the Arab Renaissance of the 8th to 12th centuries, broadly speaking, the Arab world has looked increasingly inwards upon itself. In the 1,000 years since the reign of the Caliph Mamoun, say the authors, the Arabs have translated as many books from foreign languages as Spain translates in one year. Arabs, who once led the world in science, are dropping ever further behind in scientific research, and investment in research and development is less than one-seventh of the world average. There has also been a dearth of creativity and the reports comment sadly on the shortage of new writing, and the decline in the film industry.

Gender Deficit - All outsiders are aware of the difficulties women face in Arab societies. Female illiteracy is still high and participation in economic and political life is correspondingly low. Women in Arab countries suffer from unequal citizenship and legal entitlements, compounded by an indifference towards women's desire to be allowed to get on in the world. This is an enormous waste of talent and resources.

Faith Surplus - Whereas Islam supports great values of justice, peace, tolerance, harmony on the other hand many secularists believe that the continuing Islamisation of societies over the last 20 years has played a significant part in stifling constructive Arab thought. From their schooldays onwards, Arabs are instructed that they should not defy tradition, that they should respect authority and that truth should be sought in the text and not in experience. This merely adds to the restrictions on Arab youth who find in Islam a modicum of self-respect, but also a platform for venting their frustration and anger at the outside world.-scapegoating the Western world when, as the UN report argues, the Arab world should be going about the business of changing itself.

Tunisia - It is not by chance that the present Arab awakening sparked into life in Tunisia. Together with Turkey, and symbolised by the banning of female headscarves in public, 'the State' has been firmly in charge of the struggle between State and Mosque. Tunisia was the first Arab state to have a constitution in the 19th century, the first Arab country to establish a trade union, and the first Arab country to have Arab and African human rights organizations.

Through a strong feminist movement that has existed for over a hundred years, Tunisia has always taken the lead in the Arab world on women's rights. The abolishment of polygamy and repudiation through the Code du Statut Personnel (Personal Status Code - 1956), remains an exception in the Arab world. Tunisian women were among the first in the Arab countries to obtain the right to vote in 1956. Abortion has been a full right since 1973. Access to contraceptive pills is also guaranteed.

In the current situation in Tunisia, there is a huge battle to ensure that full gender equality is enshrined in the new Constitution. Different political factions attach different priorities to the gender issue and although Ennahda, the party in government states : 'Hijab (headscarf) will become legal in all areas of life in Tunisia, and will be a personal choice. Women will retain their right to wear whatever they want, including Bikinis'. Nevertheless backsliding is an ever present possibility, as in the conservative dictum : ' Political transition first, women's rights later' Gradually, Tunisian women are making their debut on the political scene, solidifying their hard-won gains. These committed women will pave the way for younger women who may someday become policymakers without facing any obstacles because of their gender.

The struggle in Tunisia is about protecting the rights and freedoms that their citizens already have. Against the rising tide of Islamisation, this may not be easy to achieve.

Pharmacy Students   Rue du Fort, Mahdia   Oct 21

Where Is This Going ?   Medina, Kairouan   Oct 20

Running For Office   NPP Supporters, Election 2012, Elmina   Nov 20

ghana   november

Old Colonial   Bekwai, Ashanti   Nov 23

We Will Win   NDC Campaign , Kumasi   Nov 24

Activists   NPP Campaign, Kumasi   Nov 25

Shanty Town   Kronum, Kumasi, Ashanti   Nov 25

With some allowances for the holding of elections in a developing country, the 2012 General Election in Ghana was the sixth successive democratic election in Ghana. The National Democratic Congress (NDC) under Jerry John Rawlings won power in 1992 and 1996, in 2008 under John Atta Mills and narrowly under John Dramani Mahama in 2012. The New Patriotic Party (NPP) under John Agyekum Kufuor won the elections in 2000 and 2004, which meant that there were democratic transfers of political power in Ghana in 2000 and 2008. The two main parties in 2012 (NDC & NPP) accounted for 98.4% of the votes cast in a 79.4% turnout of the electorate.

The Incumbent   NDC Campaign, Tema   Nov 19

Urban   Dansoman Estates, Accra   Nov 18

Suburban   Legon, Accra   Nov 26

Consumers   Container Depot, Tema, Accra   Nov 19

Shopping   Legon, Accra   Nov 26

Modernity   Nkrumah Circle, Accra   Nov 17

Dreams   Oxford Street, Accra   Nov 18

T I A - This Is Africa   Outskirts, Cape Coast   Nov 20

Nothing has changed the prospects of Africa more than the mobile phone. Not only has there been a huge technological leapfrog into the 21st century, but non cash based payment systems also help to make Africa a little less corrupt. With its intelligent, orderly, principled population, Ghana is well placed to take full advantage of the new opportunities.

Kenya is the acknowledged technological leader in Africa and Nairobi is emerging as a sub-Saharan tech-hub, attracting top international IT companies. Safaricom in Kenya has 19 m subscribers out of a population of 43m, of which 15m use the M-Pesa mobile money transfer system for paying anything from electricity bills to school fees, thanks to a simple text based menu accessible on the most basic of mobile phones. Safaricom is developing a mobile microfinance savings and loans scheme, based on the withdrawal or transfer of cash through its existing network of 40,000 agents across the country. Mobile technology based Equity Bank has 54 products for today's customers and Microsoft has just brought out a solar powered third world smart phone. Africa is on the move!

'The person who invented the cloud did it for Africa'

Hang Out Guys   Dansoman, Accra   Nov 17

Top Up Girls   Tema, Accra   Nov 19

Courtyard   Besease, Ashanti   Nov 24

Water Pump   Jukwa, Central Region   Nov 21

African Scene   City Centre, Cape Coast   Nov 20

Planet Football   Essumeja, Ashanti   Nov 23

Palm Oil   Bekwai, Ashanti   Nov 23

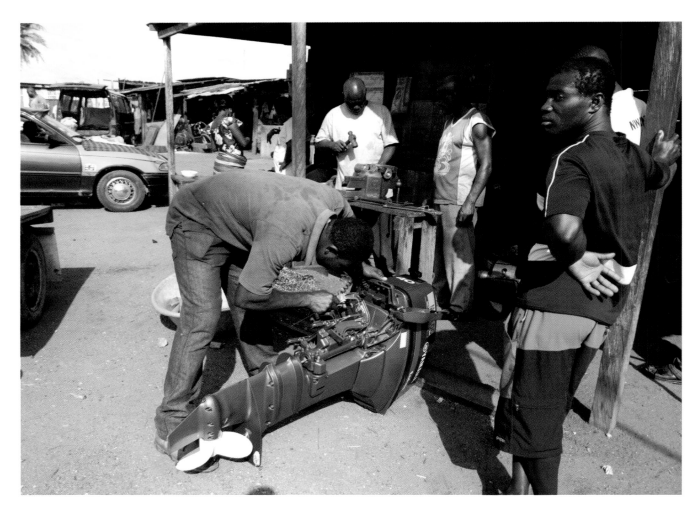

Mechanics   Elmina, Central Region   Nov 21

Timber Yard   Kumasi, Ashanti   Nov 24

Machinists   Kumasi, Ashanti   Nov 23

Drying Cocoa Beans   Jukwa, Central Region   Nov 21

African Girl   Elmina, Central Region   Nov 21

Fish Trays   Elmina, Central Region   Nov 20

Smoking Fish   Elmina, Central Region   Nov 21

Landing Fish   Elmina, Central Region   Nov 21

Market Queens   Elmina, Central Region   Nov 21

Fish Market   Elmina, Central Region   Nov 21

God World   Elmina, Central Region   Nov 21

Congregation   Kronum, Kumasi, Ashanti   Nov 25

Spirit Of Christ

Kronum, Kumasi, Ashanti

Nov 25

Dance For The Lord   Kronum, Kumasi, Ashanti   Nov 25

Prayer   Kronum, Kumasi, Ashanti   Nov 25

Witnessing   Kronum, Kumasi, Ashanti   Nov 25

Jesus Saves!   Besease, Ashanti   Nov 24

God Things   Dansoman, Accra   Nov 18

Funeral   Besease, Ashanti   Nov 24

Mr Bass Player   233 Club, North Ridge, Accra   Nov 17

The Cool Joint   233 Club, North Ridge, Accra   Nov 17

Africa's Gift To The World   233 Club, North Ridge, Accra   Nov 17

Consciousness   Cerro Tololo Observatory, La Serena, Chile   Dec 15

'Our journey to the stars is truly a journey to the heart of what we are'

Cerro Tololo Commentary

patagonia   december

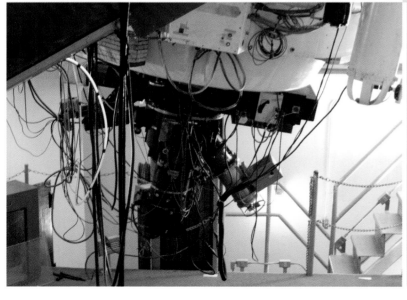

The World And Knowledge

The Privilege Of Today

Over preceding centuries, the slow accumulative advances in science and technology had gradually revealed the nature and extent of the Universe in which we exist. In the mid-1920s, the point had been reached at which the American astronomer Edwin Hubble could declare that there were other galaxies outside the Milky Way and that the Universe was expanding. His findings fundamentally changed the scientific view of the Universe, that the Universe consisted only of the Milky Way galaxy.

Launched into a low Earth orbit of 350 miles altitude in 1990, the 2.4 meter aperture Hubble Space Telescope has entirely vindicated the astronomer's findings, not to mention the stunning pictures of billions of galaxies that have been sent back to Earth. We certainly do not know everything there is to know, but as our awareness has reached even unto the background radiation of the Universe, what we can fairly safely say is that we now know where we are, in the solar system, in our own galaxy the Milky Way and in the vast spaces of the Universe. It is both extraordinary and terrifying. It is incredibly beautiful.

Of course, pure, impartial scientific 'Knowledge' can be perverted by ideological, partisan forces intent on the destruction of life, the planet or the basic human right to knowledge. But overwhelmingly, the incredible advances in science, engineering and technology have opened up immense vistas of consciousness for all present day human beings. Had we been living only a hundred years ago, we would have had a much more restricted view of the Universe by comparison. There may be other Universes to discover in succeeding centuries but it looks as if we have at least mapped out the one in which we find ourselves.

Space

'there is absolutely no prospect that any human being will ever visit
the edge of our own solar system..... ever'   Bill Bryson - 2003

There are some tough numbers to get one's head round. The speed of light, at 670 million miles per hour, is 17,000 times faster than the fastest spaceship at 39,000 mph / 11 miles per second - it takes about two years for a spaceship to cover the distance that light travels in one hour. This means it would take 73,000 years to travel the 25,000 trillion miles to the nearest star outside of our solar system, Alpha Centauri, a mere 'round the corner' 4.3 light years away. And in scientific discussions of the Universe, it is quite normal to talk in terms of millions of light years !

Although in theory, one could approach the speed of light, according to Special Relativity, the mass of an object increases as its speed increases. That mass approaches infinity as the object's speed approaches the speed of light. This means that it would take an infinite amount of energy to accelerate an object to the speed of light. Any solution to this dilemma is far in the future.

As regards our extraordinary 'Home', for the time being, perhaps even forever, we may have to be content to be observers, rather than travellers.

Dark Energy Camera

In November 2012, the Dark Energy Camera was installed on the 1974, 4-metre wide Victor M Blanco telescope at Cerro Tololo. Roughly the size of a phone booth, the camera has 62 charged-coupled devices (570 megapixels) with unprecedented sensitivity to very red light, creating the most powerful sky-mapping machine ever available. Each snapshot will collect light from 100,000 galaxies located up to 8 billion light-years away. This wide-field survey will create detailed color images of one-eighth of the sky, or 5,000 square degrees, to discover and measure 300 million galaxies, 100,000 galaxy clusters, and 4,000 supernovae.

The Dark Energy Survey, which began in December 2012, will attempt to answer one of cosmology's greatest mysteries -- why the expansion of the universe is speeding up, rather than slowing down due to gravity. Specifically, astronomers and physicists will probe the mystery of dark energy, the force which they believe is causing this increasing expansion of the universe.

Everyone Cry For Argentina   Las Madres Del Plaza De Mayo, Buenos Aires   Dec 27

Los Desaparecidos   Plaza De Mayo, Buenos Aires   Dec 27

Las Personas   Plaza De Mayo, Buenos Aires   Dec 27

Greater Love Hath No Woman   Plaza De Mayo, Buenos Aires   Dec 27

There was nothing dirtier than the 'disappearances' of left wing, liberal and intellectual opponents of the Argentine military junta during the 'Dirty War' of 1976-83. Estimates of 'Las Desaparecidos' vary from the official 11,000 up to the unofficial 30,000 but, as monitored by Amnesty International at the time, there is no doubt that the disappearances were an unusually brutal and gruesome abuse of power. Out of such atrocities, the concept of 'extrajudicial execution' began to be codified.

'Las Madres del Plaza de Mayo' started on 30 April 1977 as fourteen individual mothers searching for their children through legal means and by demonstrating in the Plaza de Mayo, in front of the Casa Rosada presidential palace. By the following year, hundreds were participating and gathering in the Plaza. The Thursday demonstrations of Las Madres have continued uninterrupted every Thursday for the last 35 years, leading to a well funded radical social reformist movement, supporting a variety of educational and housing projects.

In so doing, the Mothers created a new form of political participation, outside the traditional party structures and based on the values of love and caring. 'Motherhood allowed them to build a bond and shape a movement without men. Men were quietly involved in support of the movement. Through this process, the women transformed themselves from 'traditional' women defined by their relationships with men (mothers, wives, daughters) into public protesters working on behalf of the whole society'. (Rita Arditi)

Greater Love Hath No Man   Cafe De Los Angelitos, Buenos Aires   Dec 27

Bob Marley, Marilyn Monroe, Rudolph Valentino, Princess Diana.....over the years we have become accustomed to great public outpourings of grief at the sudden or premature deaths of those most in the public eye. None more so than for Carlos Gardel, the undisputed leading luminary of 'El Tango', killed with fellow musicians in a plane crash at the height of his career, whilst on tour in June 1935 in Colombia.

Having recorded over 300 songs and starred in dozens of films, millions of Gardel fans throughout Latin America went into mourning. Hordes came to pay their respects as his body was taken from Colombia through New York City and through Rio de Janeiro. Thousands paid homage during the two days he lay in state in Montevideo, the city in which his mother lived at the time. Gardel's charred remains eventually reached Buenos Aires in February 1936 and the funeral procession to the Chacarita Cemetery, up seventy blocks of Avenida Corrientes, a street regarded as the spiritual heart of the tango world, attracted one of the largest crowds in the modern history of Argentina. Flowers cascaded over the horse drawn carriage all along the route The government, in deference to the popular mood, decreed that for twenty-four hours no tangos were played, sung or danced anywhere in the republic.

Gardel was adored by all segments of society and his image and voice have remained unaltered, suspended in space for eternity, along with his smile, attractive face, peculiar hairdo, and his tuxedo. Even today, many years after his airplane crash, flowers and candles are lit daily at his resting place and people still say "that he sings better every passing day".

Argentina On A Friday Night   Milonga Parakultural, Buenos Aires   Dec 28

El Tango   Cafe De Los Angelitos, Buenos Aires   Dec 27

Las Casas   Coquimba, Chile   Dec 16

Back And Beyond   Y-290, Puerto Natales, Patagonia   Dec 22

Lupinos   Ruta 9 , Puerto Natales, Patagonia   Dec 22

Don't Mention The War   El Chalten, Patagonia   Dec 24

Felices Fiestas　　　　　　　　El Chalten, Patagonia　　　　　　　　Dec 24

Estancia   Nibepo Aike, El Calafate, Patagonia   Dec 25

Untethered   Nibepo Aike, El Calafate, Patagonia   Dec 25

One does not have to travel far in Argentina to witness its great love of horses and its stunningly beautiful steeds. Originating over two thousand years ago in Persia and picked up by the British in India in the early 19th century, the sport of Polo spread like wildfire among the skilful gauchos as soon as the first polo club opened in Buenos Aires in 1875. Argentina are the reigning world champions and the country is the acknowledged mecca of world polo.

Polo ponies, actually full-sized horses from 14.2 to 16 hands weighing 900–1100 lbs, are carefully selected for quick bursts of speed, stamina, and agility. Temperament is critical, the horse must remain responsive under pressure and not become excited or difficult to control. Starting at three years of age, a well trained horse will carry its rider smoothly and swiftly to the ball and can account for 60 to 75 percent of the player's skill and net worth to his team. Without any accidents, polo ponies may have the ability to play until they are 18 to 20 years of age. Outstanding polo horses are difficult to find and hugely expensive - each world class rider may have dozens and the best may cost over $200,000.

Since the first cloning of a polo pony in 2010, the technique has taken off - a three month old clone of Adolfo Cambiaso's 'Cuartetera' fetched $800,000 at auction. And after a successful career on the American polo circuit, Martin Aguerre's 'Califa', considered to be polo pony royalty, produced a clone which Aguerre described as : "....surprised how much he looks like Califa, the position of his neck, hind end and even expression in his face is so much like the original.... his mother, Luna, was one of the greatest broodmares of all time.... the whole family line is very strong."

373

Patagonian Traffic Jam   Punta Bandera, Patagonia   Dec 25

Lovely Lady Chestnut Hair Seeks Companion　　　Glaciar Viedma, Patagonia　　　Dec 24

We're Also Here   Guanacos, Torres Del Paine, Patagonia   Dec 21

Me Too !   Y-290, Puerto Natales, Patagonia   Dec 22

And Us !   Golfo Almirante Montt, Patagonia   Dec 22

Scene I   Parque Nacional Torres Del Paine, Patagonia   Dec 20

Scene II   Parque Nacional Torres Del Paine, Patagonia   Dec 20

Scene III   Parque Nacional Torres Del Paine, Patagonia   Dec 21

Torres   Parque Nacional Torres Del Paine, Patagonia   Dec 21

Room With A View   Design Suites, Lago Argentino, Patagonia   Dec 24

Wildflowers   Nibepo Aike, El Calafate, Patagonia   Dec 25

Ice   Glaciar Perito Moreno, El Calafate, Patagonia   Dec 23

Space I   Lago Viedma, El Chalten, Patagonia   Dec 24

Space II   Esperanza, Patagonia   Dec 23

The House Lights Go Down   Lago Argentino, El Calafate, Patagonia   Dec 25

Ready For The Show   El Calafate, Patagonia   Dec 25

Galaxy - NASA, ESA, J. GaBany and R. Gendler, Hubble Heritage Team

Ultra Deep Field - NASA, ESA, S. Beckwith (STScI) and the HUDF Team

Love the world

' In all true love, there is the love of the Infinite in the person or thing we love '

Juan Mascaro   Introduction : Bhagavad Gita   1962

other works

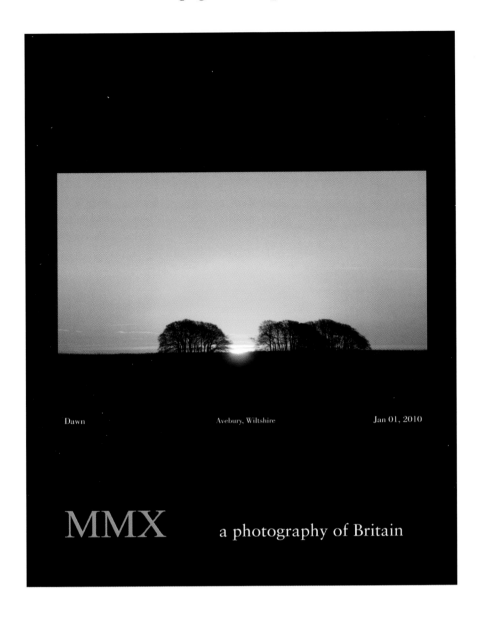

The first volume of an ambitious three part publication to document the life of Britain
at the turn of the first three decades of the 21st century.

'Thank you very much for an amazing book.' Labour MP

'We are delighted to accept it for our members to enjoy.'   National Liberal Club

'Many thanks for sending me your fascinating and beautifully illustrated book.' Conservative MP

'It has certainly made me feel more positive about where I live.' Nick W - Landscape Architect

'A masterpiece, a work of high art. The feeling of seeing things as they are permeates every page.
I absolutely love it.' James S - Spiriitual Teacher

' I have a reasonably large collection of photo-essays by photographers ranging from Ansel Adams,
Walker Evans and Margaret Bourke-White through to Sebastiao Salgado, and this is right up there
with the best.' Sid V - Amateur Photographer

'Shishu'
Japanese Garden Culture
DVD 53mins

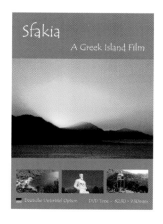

'Sfakia'
Greek Island Life
DVD 72mins

'The Unchanging Self'
Indian Spiritual Culture
DVD 67mins

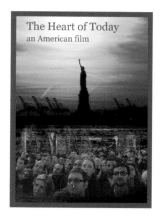

'The Heart Of Today'
a film about New York & Democracy
DVD 124mins

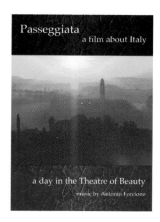

'Passeggiata'
a film about Italy
DVD 70mins

'God, Chocolate &
The Black Stars'
contemporary African culture
DVD 49mins

'Sen Shin An'
the other world of Japanese Tea
DVD 55mins / Bluray 67mins

www.inspirita.org